Contents

CITY COLLEGE MANCHESTER

00129488

Chapter 1
What is a spreadsheet?

Getting started

A **spreadsheet** is a very useful piece of computer software mainly used for working with numbers. Spreadsheets are used in thousands of different applications which involve doing calculations or drawing charts on data such as, for example:

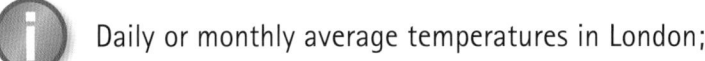 Daily or monthly average temperatures in London;

Marks for a class of pupils;

Times of runners in a race;

 Amount of money spent on books, equipment, teachers, trips, etc. in a school.

Spreadsheets are often used for planning budgets and working with financial data. Different figures can be entered and the effect of the changes will be calculated automatically.

Microsoft Excel is one of many different spreadsheet packages. In Excel, spreadsheets are referred to as **workbooks**. Just to make it even more confusing, a workbook can contain several **worksheets**.

In this chapter you will learn how to move around a worksheet and enter text and numbers.

Load **Microsoft Excel.** You can do this in one of two ways:

 Either double-click the **Excel** icon ————————————

Microsoft
Excel

 Or click **Start** at the bottom left of the screen, then click **Programs, Microsoft Office,** then click

Microsoft Excel

Note:
If you are using Excel 2000 you will not see the **Task pane** on the right of the screen.

Your screen will look like the one below:

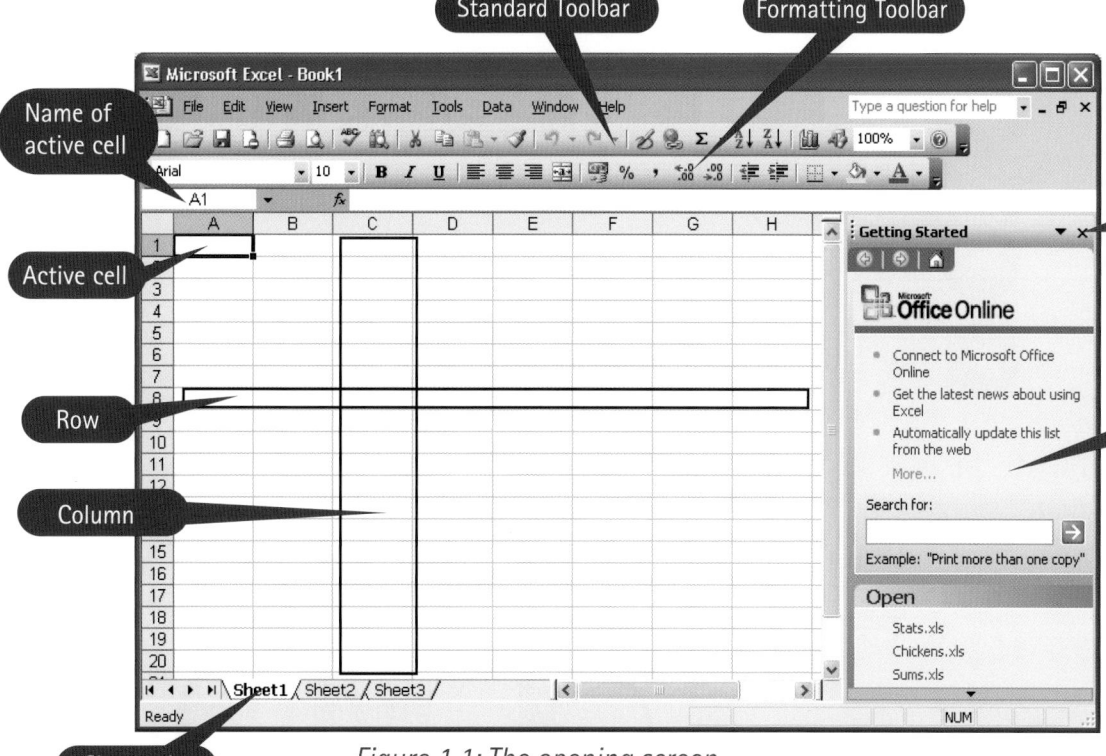

Standard Toolbar

Formatting Toolbar

Name of active cell

Click here to close the Task Pane

Active cell

Row

Task Pane

Column

Sheet tabs

Figure 1.1: The opening screen

 A worksheet contains 256 **columns** and 16,384 **rows.** You can only see a few of these on the screen.

 The **columns** are labelled A, B, C and so on. The **rows** are labelled 1, 2, 3 etc.

Note:
The Task pane is new in Excel 2002. It lists the workbooks you recently opened and other options. Close it now by clicking on the X at the top of the Task Pane.

 The worksheet is divided into **cells** in which you can type a number, a label or a formula. The address of the cell in the top left hand corner is **A1,** because it is in column **A** and row **1.**

 A **workbook** contains several blank **worksheets** named **Sheet1, Sheet2, Sheet3** etc. These names are on the **sheet tabs** shown in Figure 1.1.

Moving around the worksheet

When you open a new workbook, cell A1 is highlighted, showing that it is the **active cell.** When you start typing, the letters or numbers will appear in this cell.

You can move around the spreadsheet to make a cell active in any of these ways:

 Move the pointer using the mouse and click the left mouse button in the cell you want.

 Use one of the arrow keys to go up, down, left or right.

 Use the **Page Up** or **Page Down** keys.

Note:

Notice that when you leave the pointer over a button on one of the toolbars at the top of the screen for a few seconds, a 'Tool Tip' appears telling you what the button does.

Experiment!

 Try moving around the spreadsheet using the arrow keys and **Page Up, Page Down** keys.

 Try holding down the **Ctrl** key while you use any of the arrow keys. What happens?

 What is the name (i.e. address or cell reference) of the very last cell in the worksheet?

 With the active cell somewhere in the middle of the worksheet, try pressing **Ctrl-Home.** Where does this take you?

Entering data

Suppose your school has a fete or Fun Day coming up, and everyone in your class has been asked to sell some books of raffle tickets. Your job is to make a list of the number of books that each pupil has taken home.

The list will look like this:

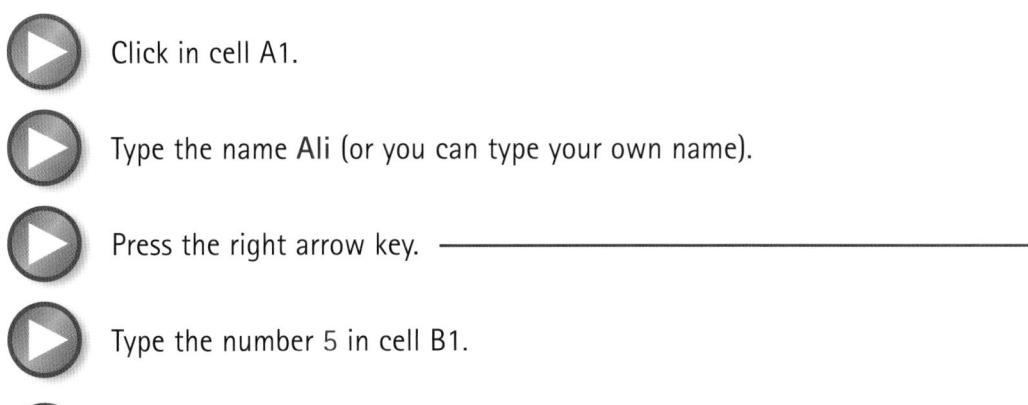

Figure 1.2

Click in cell A1.

Type the name Ali (or you can type your own name).

Press the right arrow key.

Type the number 5 in cell B1.

Press **Enter. Excel** guesses that you are typing a list and goes to cell A2. (If it does not, click in A2 or use the arrow keys to go there.)

Copy the rest of the list. If you make any mistakes, it doesn't matter. You can correct them in a minute.

Tip:

If you start to type another name beginning with say, W in cell A7, Excel will guess that you are going to type **William** again and enter the letters for you. If you were going to type William, you can just tab out of the cell or press **Enter.** If you were going to type **Walter** or some other name beginning with W, just carry on typing. Try it out.

Editing data

One name has been spelt wrongly. It should be spelt **Clare,** not **Claire.**
There are several ways of putting it right and you can try two of them.

First way

 Click in the cell containing the name **Claire.** You will see that the
name appears in the **formula bar,** as shown below.

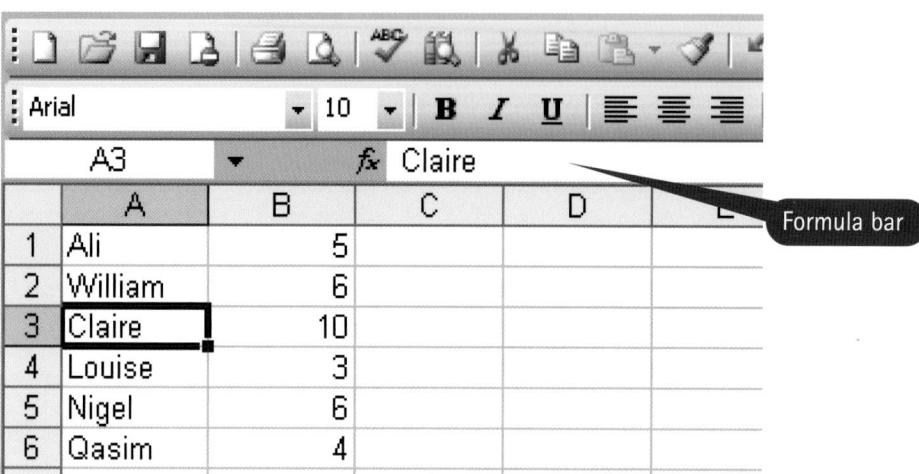

Figure 1.3

Click in the formula bar (Figure 1.3). Use the arrow keys to move the insertion
point between i and r, and then press the **Backspace** key. You will see that the
change is made in the cell A3 at the same time as you edit the name in the
formula bar.

 Press **Enter** to register the change.

Second way

Another way to edit a cell is simply to type over the text in
the cell. Suppose it was Kim, not Louise, who took 3 books
of raffle tickets.

 Click in the cell containing the name **Louise.**

 Type Kim.

 Press **Enter.**

Deleting the contents of a cell

To delete the contents of a cell, click in the cell and then press the **Delete** key on the keyboard.

 Delete the name **Nigel.**

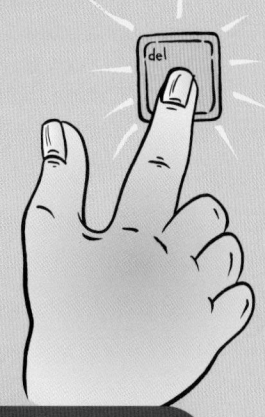

Warning!

If you press the **Space** bar instead of pressing the **Delete** key, the cell will appear to be empty but it is not – it contains a **Space** character. This can cause problems, so always use the **Delete** key to delete the contents of a cell.

Inserting and deleting rows and columns

We can delete the whole of Row 5 so that no gap is left between **Kim** and **Qasim.**

 Right-click the row header for row 5 (see below in Figure 1.4).

 Select **Delete** from the shortcut menu which appears.

 Click the left mouse button.

The entry for **Qasim** moves up to Row 5.

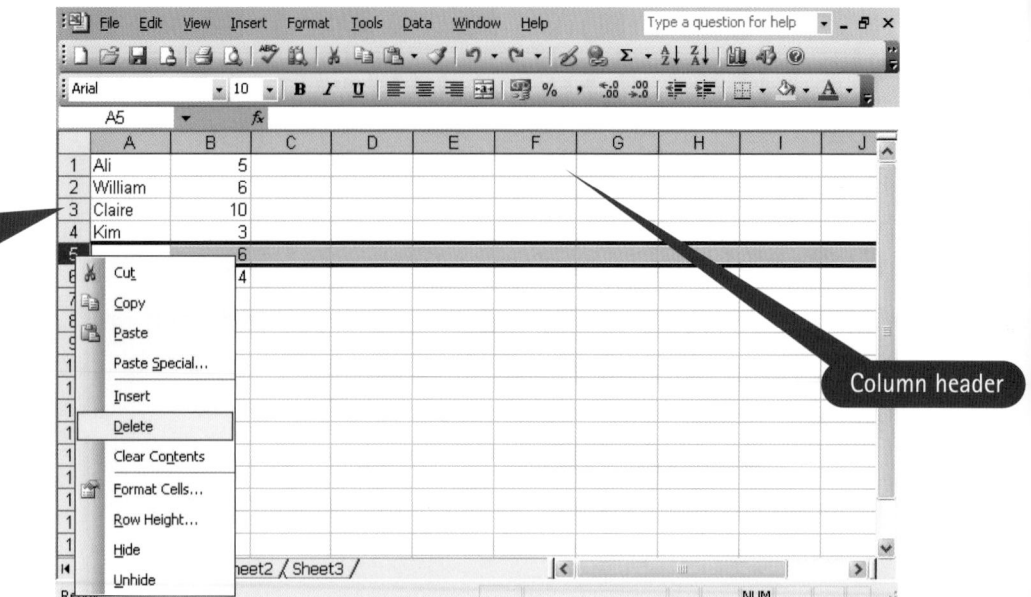

The numbers 1, 2, 3... down the side of the worksheet are called **row headers.** Right-click 5 to select Row 5 and display the shortcut menu.

Column header

Figure 1.4

Tip:

You can insert and delete columns in the same way, by right-clicking a column header and selecting **Insert** or **Delete** from the shortcut menu. Try inserting a new column between columns A and B, and then deleting it again.

Now suppose we want to put a heading at the top of the worksheet, above the names. We need to insert a new row.

▶ Right-click the row header for row 1.

▶ Select **Insert** from the shortcut menu.

▶ Click the left mouse button.

▶ Type Raffle Tickets in cell A1 of the new row. Press **Enter.**

▶ Insert another blank line below the header. (No help this time!)

Saving your work

Tip:

If you don't see **Save,** click the double arrow at the bottom of the **File** menu to see more options.

If you want to keep your work so that you can add to it or change it another day, you must save it.

▶ Click **File** on the main menu, and then click **Save.** You'll see a screen rather like Figure 1.5.

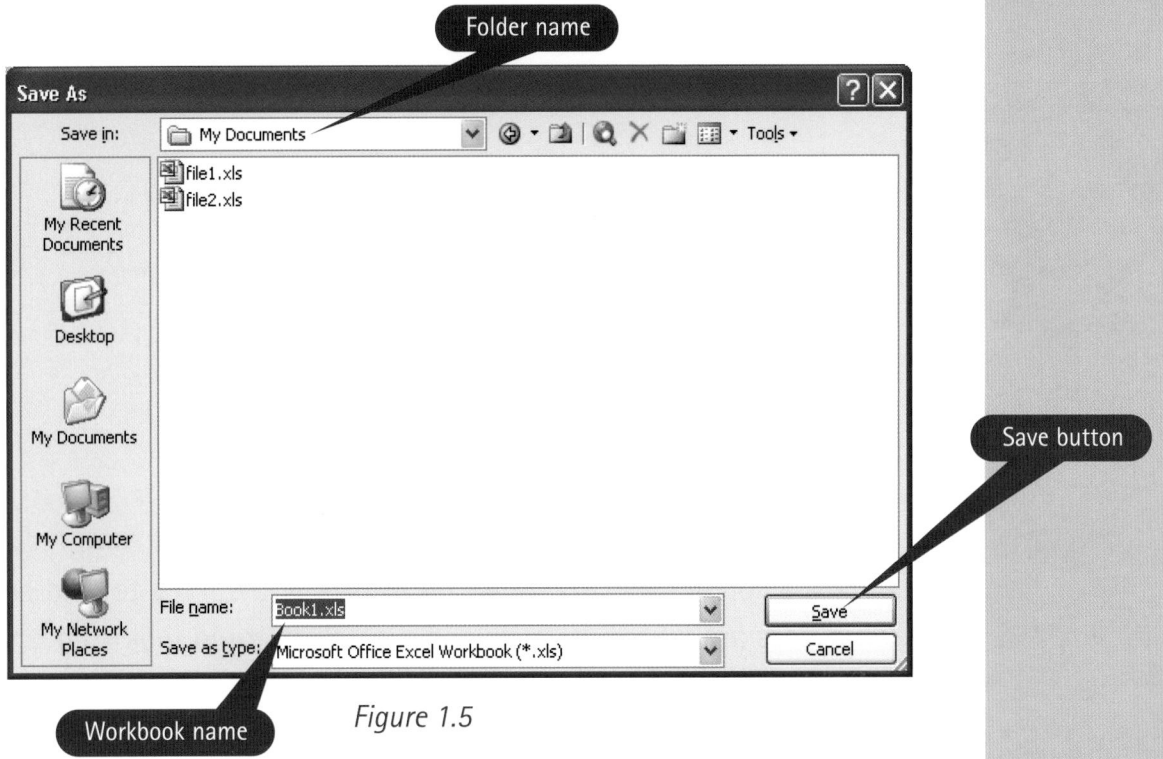

Figure 1.5

Excel gives your workbook the default name **Book1.xls.** The name appears in the **File name** box.

The name will be highlighted to show that it is selected ready for you to change it if you want to.

When text is selected you don't have to delete it before typing over it.

 Type a new name, Raffle Tickets.

Microsoft Excel will add an **extension** (a full stop and the three letters **xls**) to the name you choose. This shows that the file is a spreadsheet created using **Microsoft Excel.**

Your teacher may need to show you in which folder to save your file. In the screenshot above, the workbook will be saved in a folder called **My Documents.**

Tip:
Look at the top of your screen. You will see the name **Raffle Tickets.xls.** This tells you that your work will be saved with this name any time you click the **Save** button.

 Click the **Save** button. This saves your document and automatically closes the dialogue box.

 Close your workbook by selecting **File** from the main menu. Then click **Close.**

Additional Exercise

Create a spreadsheet to show the results of a survey to find out what pets are owned by pupils in a class. It could look something like this:

	A	B	C	D	E	F	G	H
1	Survey of Pets		Class:		Name:			
2								
3	Name		Dog	Cat	Rabbit	Hamster	Gerbil	Horse
4	David		2					
5	Rebecca				1		1	
6	Edward							
7	Jasmine			2				1
8	Chloe							
9	Lee		1					
10	Anton						1	
11								

Figure 1.6

Save the spreadsheet with the name **Pet Survey.**

Chapter **2**
Formulae

The real fun with spreadsheets starts with **formulae.** Using a formula **Excel** will perform calculations for you automatically.

To find out how formulae work in **Excel,** we'll start by doing a page of 'sums'. We'll be using the following mathematical symbols:

+	(add)
-	(subtract)
*	(multiply)
/	(divide)
( )	(brackets are used whenever necessary)

The first task will be to set out the page just the way we want it.

Project: Create a worksheet to do calculations

	A	B	C	D	E	F	G	H
1	ADD		SUBTRACT		DIVIDE		MULTIPLY	
2	100		100		230		57.3	
3	400		56		14.5		12.5	
4								
5								
6								

Figure 2.1: A page of sums ready for entering formulae

▶ Open a new **Excel** workbook.

▶ Type the text ADD, SUBTRACT, DIVIDE, MULTIPLY in cells A1, C1, E1 and G1 as shown in Figure 2.1.

▶ Type all the numbers as shown in the correct cells.

Selecting cells

In order to format the text in certain cells by making it bold or changing the font, the cells first have to be **selected.** Try the following ways to select a range of cells:

▶ Click in the intersection of the row and column headers to select every cell in the worksheet. All the selected cells appear highlighted.

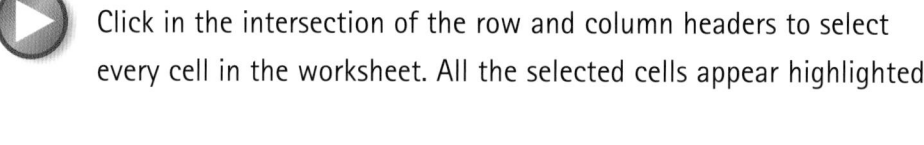

Click here to select the whole worksheet

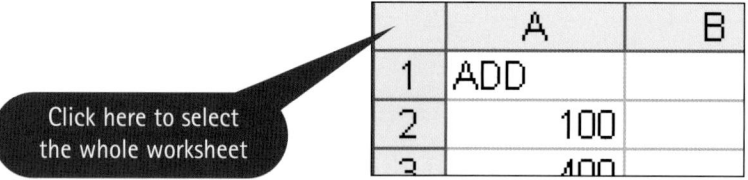

Figure 2.2: Selecting the whole worksheet

▶ Click in column header A to select column A. The new selection replaces the previous one.

▶ Click in row header 1 to select row 1.

▶ Drag the mouse across cells A1 to G1 to select those cells.

▶ To select just cells A1, C1, E1 and G1, click in cell A1 and then hold down the **Ctrl** key while you click each of the other cells.

Making text bold

You can format text in a worksheet in a similar way to a document created in **Word.**

 Make sure cells A1 to G1 are selected.

 Press the **Bold** button on the Formatting toolbar. ———————————— **B**

Inserting a border

Cells A4, C4, E4 and G4 need a thick top and bottom border.

 Click cell A4. Hold down **Ctrl** while you click each of the other cells to select them.

 From the main menu select **Format, Cells...**

 A dialogue box should appear. Click the **Border** tab.

Note:
In some versions of Excel you cannot make borders as described below, so you may have to do without borders. In this case, save your work as **Sums** and go on to Entering Formulae on the next page.

The dialogue box will look something like the one below:

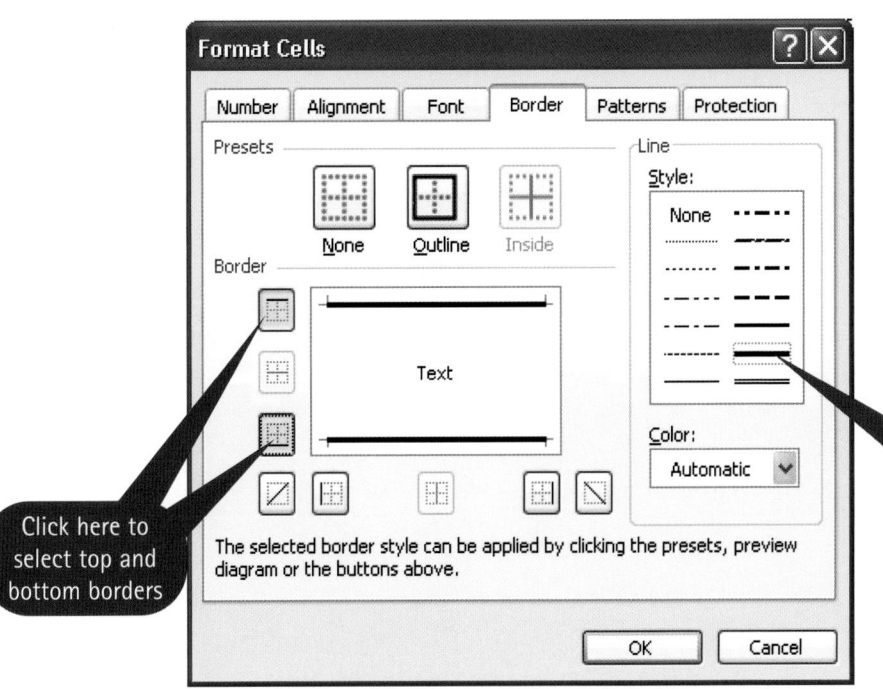

Figure 2.3: Selecting cell borders

 Select the line style by clicking a thick line in the **Style** box as shown above.

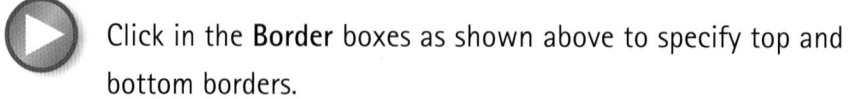 Click in the **Border** boxes as shown above to specify top and bottom borders.

 Click **OK.**

▶ Click away from the cells and you will see that all the cells you selected now have a top and bottom border.

	A	B	C	D	E	F	G	H
1	ADD		SUBTRACT		DIVIDE		MULTIPLY	
2	100		100		230		57.3	
3	400		56		14.5		12.5	
4								
5								
6								

Figure 2.4

▶ Before you do any more work, save the workbook, naming it **Sums.**

Entering formulae

Formulae are entered using cell references.

▶ Click in cell A4.

▶ Type an equals sign (=) to tell **Excel** that you are about to enter a formula.

▶ Type a2+a3 so that the formula appears as shown below.

SUM	▾ ✗ ✓ *fx*	=a2+a3		
	A	B	C	D
1	**ADD**		**SUBTRACT**	
2	100		100	
3	400		56	
4	=a2+a3			
5				

Figure 2.5: Entering a formula

▶ Press **Enter.** The answer appears!

▶ In cell C4, type =c2−c3 and press **Enter**.

▶ In cell E4, type =e2/e3 and press **Enter**.

▶ In cell G4, type =g2*g3 and press **Enter**.

Now your worksheet should look like this:

	A	B	C	D	E	F	G	H
1	ADD		SUBTRACT		DIVIDE		MULTIPLY	
2	100		100		230		57.3	
3	400		56		14.5		12.5	
4	500		44		15.86207		716.25	
5								

Figure 2.6: The finished worksheet

Automatic re-calculation

The great thing about a spreadsheet is that once you have entered the formulae, you can change the contents of the other cells and the answers will still be right.

 Change cell A2 to **75.** What is the answer now?

 Delete the contents of cells C2 and C3 by selecting them and then pressing the **Delete** key. What is the answer in cell C4?

 What is 0 divided by 2? Use your spreadsheet to find out.

 What is 2.75 x 3.8? (Type 2.75 in cell G2 and 3.8 in cell G3 and you should get 10.45.)

 Do you remember that it is a bad idea to press the **Space** bar instead of the **Delete** key to delete the contents of a cell? Try doing that now in cell E2, press **Enter** and you'll see why. Your worksheet will look something like the one below.

	A	B	C	D	E	F	G	H
1	ADD		SUBTRACT		DIVIDE		MULTIPLY	
2	75						2.75	
3	400				2		3.8	
4	475		0		#VALUE!		10.45	
5								

This is caused by typing a space in cell E2 instead of deleting its contents

Figure 2.7

 Delete the space in cell E2. Now the answer should be 0.

 Try putting 0 in cell E3. This will give you a different error message in E4, **#DIV/0!** Why do you think that is?

Tip:
You can undo your last action by pressing the **Undo** button

Entering formulae by pointing

Instead of typing in a formula such as **=a2+a3** you can use the mouse to point to the cells in the formula.

 Restore the worksheet to how it looks in Figure 2.4. Delete the formulae in row 4.

 In cell A4, type = and then click the mouse in cell A2.

 Type + and then click the mouse in cell A3.

 Press **Enter.**

 Try entering the other formulae in the same way.

 When you have finished experimenting, save your workbook again.

Additional exercise

You have 100m of chicken wire to enclose an area for the chickens.

Use a spreadsheet to carry out an investigation into the maximum area you can enclose with the available chicken wire.

Your spreadsheet might look something like this:

Tip:

You can make column A wider by dragging the line between column headings A and B to the right.

	A	B	C	D	E	F	G
1	Fencing in the chickens						
2							
3	Perimeter	100		This is the amount of chicken wire available			
4							
5	**Length**	**30**					
6	Length x 2	60		The formula in cell B6 is =2*B5			
7	Wire left over for sides	40		The formula in cell B6 is =100-B6			
8							
9	**Breadth**	20		The formula in cell B8 is =B7/2			
10							
11							
12	**Area (Length x Breadth)**	600		The formula in cell B12 is =B5*B9			
13							

Figure 2.8

If you put the right formulae in cells B6, B7, B9 and B12 you can try out different values in B5 to see which dimensions give you the maximum area. What is the answer?

Chapter **3**
Columns of Data

You're just beginning to find out all the wonders of a spreadsheet! Next you'll find out how to control the way numbers are displayed, and make **Excel** automatically calculate column totals.

Project: Create a spreadsheet to hold data about the height, weight and foot size of pupils in the class.

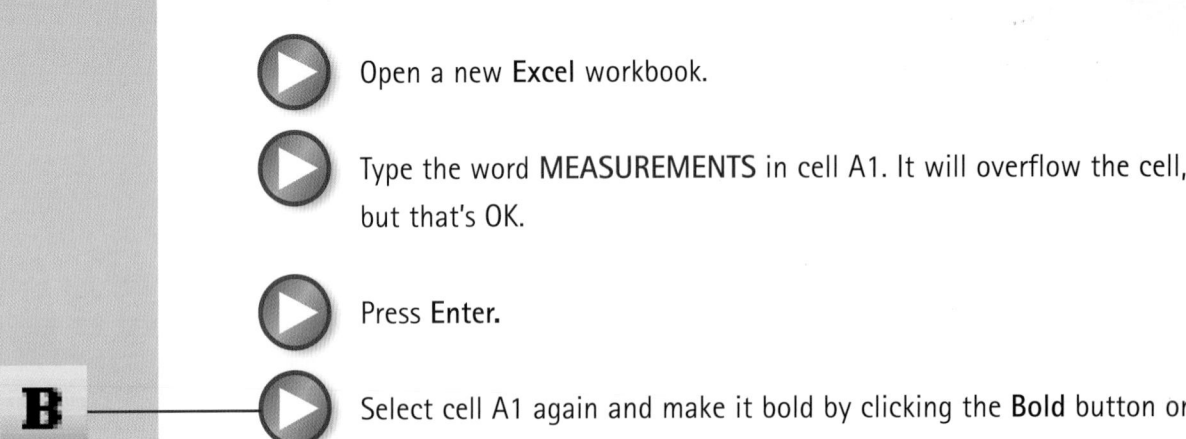

▶ Open a new **Excel** workbook.

▶ Type the word **MEASUREMENTS** in cell A1. It will overflow the cell, but that's OK.

▶ Press **Enter.**

▶ Select cell A1 again and make it bold by clicking the **Bold** button on the Formatting toolbar.

Changing column widths

You can change the width of column A so that the word MEASUREMENTS fits into cell A1.

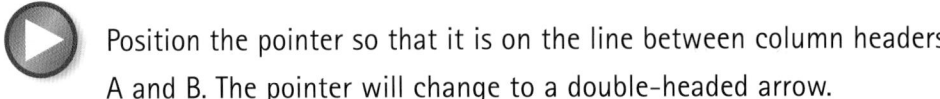 Position the pointer so that it is on the line between column headers A and B. The pointer will change to a double-headed arrow.

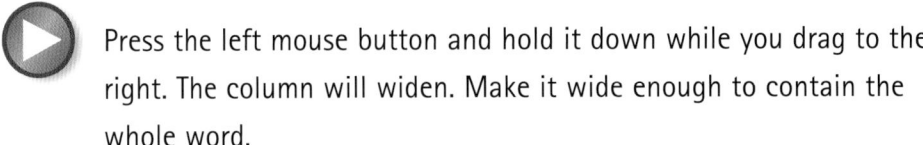 Press the left mouse button and hold it down while you drag to the right. The column will widen. Make it wide enough to contain the whole word.

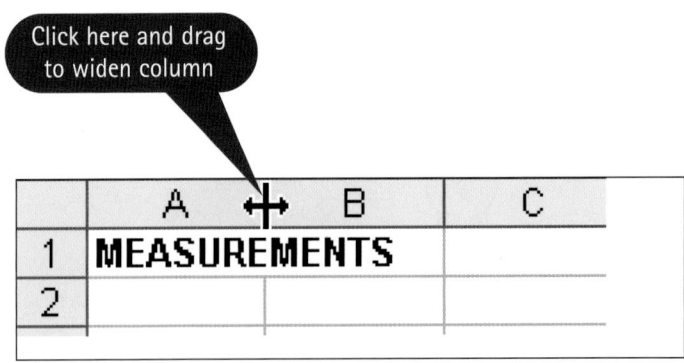

Figure 3.1: Widening a column

Now type the other headings in the top line as shown in Figure 3.2. Type your own class and name instead of **6R, Frances Lake.**

Now try a second way of widening a column.

 Position the pointer between the column headers of columns F and G containing your name.

 Double-click. The column automatically widens so that the name will fit in the cell.

 Save your workbook, calling it **Stats** (short for Statistics).

Tip:
This is called **autosizing** the cell width.

Formatting numbers

 Now fill in the rest of the headings, names and data.

	A	B	C	D	E	F
1	MEASUREMENTS		CLASS 6R		Name:	Frances Lake
2						
3	Name	Height(cm)	Weight(kg)	Foot length(cm)		
4	Anthony Goddard	131.5	35.3	19.5		
5	Timothy Salter	126	30	18.4		
6	Kerry Meredith	138	39.5	21		
7	Deborah Roberts	129.7	34.8	18.3		
8	Hussen Shah	132.5	33	20.3		
9	Touqir Mylas	130	34	19		
10						
11	TOTAL					
12						
13	AVERAGE					
14						
15	MAXIMUM					
16						
17	MINIMUM					
18						

Figure 3.2

You'll notice that data starting with a letter (A, B, C etc) is automatically **left-justified** in a cell. Numeric data on the other hand is automatically **right-justified.**

Tip:
It is nearly always best to leave numbers right-justified so that the decimal points, units, tens, hundreds etc line up. If necessary, you can right-justify column headings so they line up over the numbers.

The measurements in the screenshot (Figure 3.2) would look much neater if they were all shown to 1 decimal place. You'll find if you enter **126.0,** Excel ignores the part after the decimal point and displays **126** instead.

To cure this the numbers need to be **formatted.** There is a quick way of doing this.

Select cells B4 to D17 by dragging across them.

Click the **Increase Decimal** button on the Formatting toolbar.

Note:
If you do not see the **Increase Decimal** and **Decrease Decimal** buttons on your toolbar, you can select **Format, Cells,** from the menu and click the **Number** tab. Then select **Number** from the list and set the number of decimal places.

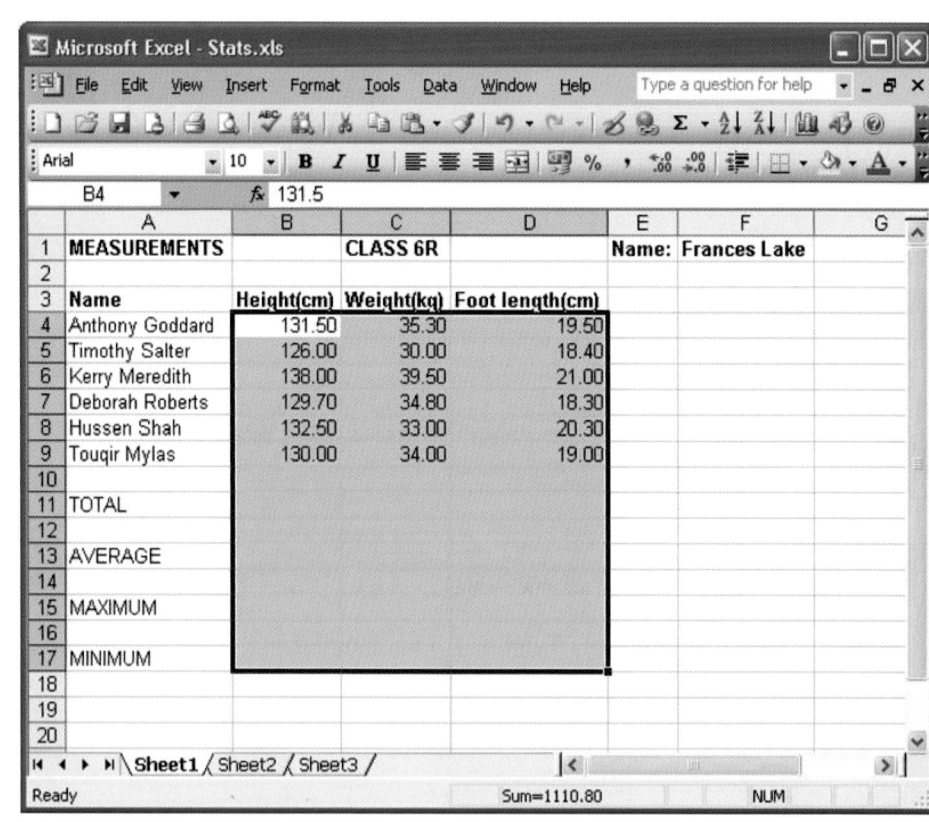

Figure 3.3

Now click the **Decrease Decimal** button to display all the numbers to 1 decimal place.

Save your workbook again. A quick way to do this is to press **Ctrl-S.** You should do this every few minutes!

Adding a column of numbers

Now we want to add up the heights of everyone in the class and put the Total in cell B11. To do this we will use the **Autosum** button.

The sign Σ (pronounced **Sigma**) on the **Autosum** button is the Greek letter **S**. Have you ever been to Greece? Do you know any other Greek letters?

Greek letters are used a lot in mathematics.
π is the Greek letter p.

Area of a
circle $=\pi r^2$

 Click in cell B11 to make it the active cell.

 Click the **Autosum** button. ——————————————— Σ ▾

Excel guesses which cells you want to sum. Your screen will look like the one below.

	A	B	C	D	E	F
1	MEASUREMENTS		CLASS 6R		Name:	Frances Lake
2						
3	Name	Height(cm)	Weight(kg)	Foot length(cm)		
4	Anthony Goddard	131.5	35.3	19.5		
5	Timothy Salter	126.0	30.0	18.4		
6	Kerry Meredith	138.0	39.5	21.0		
7	Deborah Roberts	129.7	34.8	18.3		
8	Hussen Shah	132.5	33.0	20.3		
9	Touqir Mylas	130.0	34.0	19.0		
10						
11	TOTAL	=SUM(B4:B10)				
12		SUM(**number1**, [number2], ...)				
13	AVERAGE					
14						
15	MAXIMUM					
16						
17	MINIMUM					
18						

Figure 3.4

 Press **Enter.** The answer appears.

 Find the total weight in cell C11.

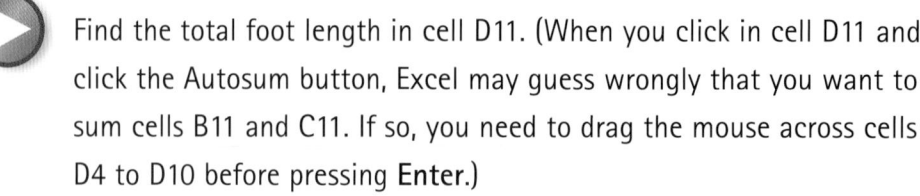 Find the total foot length in cell D11. (When you click in cell D11 and click the Autosum button, Excel may guess wrongly that you want to sum cells B11 and C11. If so, you need to drag the mouse across cells D4 to D10 before pressing **Enter.**)

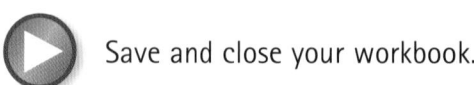 Save and close your workbook.

In the next chapter you'll use a formula to calculate the average height, weight and foot length. You will use a **function** to find the maximum and minimum values.

Additional exercise

Load the workbook **Raffle Tickets** that you created in chapter 1.

Insert new rows where necessary to add column headings.

Use the **Autosum** button to find the total number of raffle tickets issued.

Each book of tickets contains 10 tickets worth 50p each. Add a new column containing a formula giving the value of the ticket books taken by each pupil.

Use the **Autosum** button to find the total value of raffle ticket books issued.

Chapter **4**
Functions

In this chapter you will continue to work on the **Stats**
spreadsheet that you started in the last chapter. You will
be learning how to use **Excel's** built-in **functions** to calculate
the average, maximum and minimum measurements.

A function is a formula used in a calculation. **Excel** provides
over 200 functions to help with business, scientific and
engineering applications. Don't worry, you only need 3 or
4 at this stage!

 Load the spreadsheet **Stats** that you created in the last chapter.

It should look something like the one below. The **Formula bar** and
the **active cell** have been labelled in the screenshot.

	A	B	C	D	E	F	G
1	MEASUREMENTS		CLASS 6R		Name:	Frances Lake	
2							
3	Name	Height(cm)	Weight(kg)	Foot length(cm)			
4	Anthony Goddard	131.5	35.3	19.5			
5	Timothy Salter	126.0	30.0	18.4			
6	Kerry Meredith	138.0	39.5	21.0			
7	Deborah Roberts	129.7	34.8	18.3			
8	Hussen Shah	132.5	33.0	20.3			
	Mylas	130.0	34.0	19.0			
11	TOTAL	787.7	206.6	116.5			
12							
13	AVERAGE						
14							
15	MAXIMUM						
16							
17	MINIMUM						
18							

Cell B11: fx =SUM(B4:B10)

Formula bar

Active cell

Figure 4.1

25

The SUM function

You have already used a function without realising it.

Look at the **Formula bar** in the screenshot above. It tells you what formula has been used to get the answer 787.7 in the **active cell**, B11.

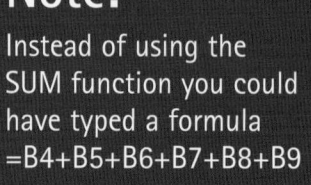

You entered the SUM function by pressing the **Autosum** button. Adding up a row or column of numbers is such a common task in spreadsheet work that this special shortcut button is provided.

You can also enter a function by typing it into the cell. We'll try that now.

 Click in cell B11.

 Press the **Delete** key. Now we can try another way of entering the SUM function.

 Type =sum(in the cell (including the opening bracket).

 Now click in cell B4 and hold the left mouse button down while you drag down to cell B10. Notice that **Excel** is automatically filling in the formula as you do this in both the cell and the formula bar.

 Type) to finish the formula.

 Press **Enter.** Click in cell B11 again and the formula =SUM(B4:B10) appears in the Formula bar as in Figure 4.1.

Note:

Instead of using the SUM function you could have typed a formula =B4+B5+B6+B7+B8+B9

Are you wondering why we included the blank cell B10 in the formula? Wait a while and you will find out!

The AVERAGE function

The AVERAGE function works in much the same way as the SUM function.

 Click in cell B13.

 Type =average(in the cell (including the opening bracket).

 Click in cell B4 and drag down to cell B10. Type) to finish the formula.

 Press **Enter.** The answer, 131.3, appears in the cell.

 In cell C13 find the average weight in the same way (It should be 34.4).

 In cell D13 find the average foot length (19.4).

Tip:
You can use either upper or lower case letters for the function name, or even a mixture of both.

MAX and MIN functions

To find the maximum, you need the MAX function.

 Click in cell B15.

 Type =max(in the cell (including the opening bracket).

 Click in cell B4 and drag down to cell B10. Type) to finish the formula.

 Press **Enter.** The answer, 138.0, appears in the cell.

 Complete the other formulas in row 15.

 Use the **MIN** function to find the minimums.

Tip:

ALWAYS check the results of formulae to make sure the answers are reasonable. If the spreadsheet tells you that your classmates have an average height of 27cm or 196cm, you need to check that you have entered the formula correctly!

Your spreadsheet will look like this:

	A	B	C	D	E	F	G
	D17	▼		f_x =MIN(D4:D10)			
1	MEASUREMENTS		CLASS 6R		Name:	Frances Lake	
2							
3	Name	Height(cm)	Weight(kg)	Foot length(cm)			
4	Anthony Goddard	131.5	35.3	19.5			
5	Timothy Salter	126.0	30.0	18.4			
6	Kerry Meredith	138.0	39.5	21.0			
7	Deborah Roberts	129.7	34.8	18.3			
8	Hussen Shah	132.5	33.0	20.3			
9	Touqir Mylas	130.0	34.0	19.0			
10							
11	TOTAL	787.7	206.6	116.5			
12							
13	AVERAGE	131.3	34.4	19.4			
14							
15	MAXIMUM	138.0	39.5	21.0			
16							
17	MINIMUM	126.0	30.0	18.3			
18							

Figure 4.2

What if?

What if you want to include another person in your list of measurements?

The first thing to do is to insert a new row after **Touqir Mylas.** Then we can insert the new name and measurements. But how will this affect the formulae for Total, Average, Max and Min?

Let's find out!

 Click the row header for row 10 with the **right** mouse button.

Right- click here

8	Hussen Shah	132.5	33.0	20.3
9	Touqir Mylas	130.0	34.0	19.0
10				
11	TOTAL	787.7	206.6	116.5

Figure 4.3

A shortcut menu appears. Select **Insert** from the menu to insert a new row.

 In the new row, enter the data for **Jacob Walton,** who is **139cm** tall, weighs **40.0kg** and has a foot length of **22.5cm.**

 Click in cell B12 and look at the formula in the formula bar. The formula has automatically adjusted to include the new row. Clever or what?

Your spreadsheet should now look like this:

	B12	▾	f_x =SUM(B4:B11)					
	A	B	C	D	E	F		G
1	MEASUREMENTS		CLASS 6R		Name:	Frances Lake		
2								
3	Name	Height(cm)	Weight(kg)	Foot length(cm)				
4	Anthony Goddard	131.5	35.3	19.5				
5	Timothy Salter	126.0	30.0	18.4				
6	Kerry Meredith	138.0	39.5	21.0				
7	Deborah Roberts	129.7	34.8	18.3				
8	Hussen Shah	132.5	33.0	20.3				
9	Touqir Mylas	130.0	34.0	19.0				
10	Jacob Walton	139.0	40.0	22.5				
11								
12	TOTAL	926.7	246.6	139.0				
13								
14	AVERAGE	132.4	35.2	19.9				
15								
16	MAXIMUM	139.0	40.0	22.5				
17								
18	MINIMUM	126.0	30.0	18.3				

Figure 4.4

If it does not, check the formulae.

If you had not included Row 10 in your formulae originally, the formulae would not have adjusted when you entered a new row. That's because the new row would be outside the range specified in the formulae.

 Save your spreadsheet and close it.

Additional exercise

Carry out your own survey of classmates. You could include other measurements such as hand size, reach and head size.

Use a spreadsheet to record the results. Do the tallest people have the biggest hands and feet? Do the heaviest people have the largest heads? Do boys weigh more than girls of the same height, or have bigger feet?

Tip:

To find the average of cells B4, B5, B8, B9 and B10 (i.e. average height of the boys) you need to enter the formula
=average(B4,B5,B8,B9,B10).

You can also enter this formula like this:

In the cell where you want the average type **=average(**

Drag across cells B4,B5 to select them.

Type a comma.

Drag across cells B8 to B10 to select them.

Type a closing bracket.

Press Enter.

The formula should say **=Average(B4:B5,B8:B10)**

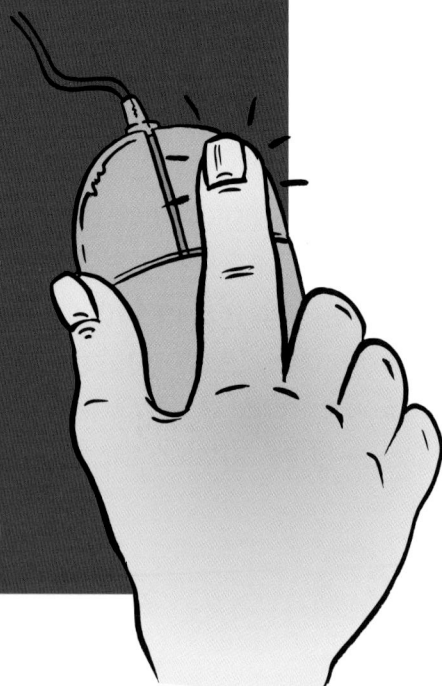

Chapter **5**
Bar Charts

Charts are a very good way of presenting information in a way that is easy to grasp immediately. 'A picture paints a thousand words', as the saying goes.

In this chapter we'll look at how the number of songbirds in the UK has declined over the past three decades.

This sad and alarming decline is partly due to modern farming methods. Many hedgerows, meadows and marshes have disappeared, so birds have nowhere to live. Chemicals sprayed on fields kill insects that birds need for food.

Project: Draw charts relating to the number of songbirds in England.

Decline in songbird numbers between 1972 and 1996 (Numbers given in millions)		
	1972	1996
Skylark	7.72	3.09
Willow warbler	6.06	4.67
Linnet	1.56	0.925
Song thrush	3.62	1.74
Lapwing	0.588	0.341
Yellowhammer	4.4	1.76
Blackbird	12.54	8.4
Tree sparrow	0.65	0.0845
Corn bunting	0.144	0.03

Source: British Trust for Ornithology

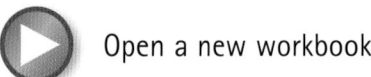 Open a new workbook.

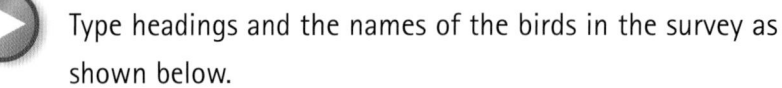 Type headings and the names of the birds in the survey as shown below.

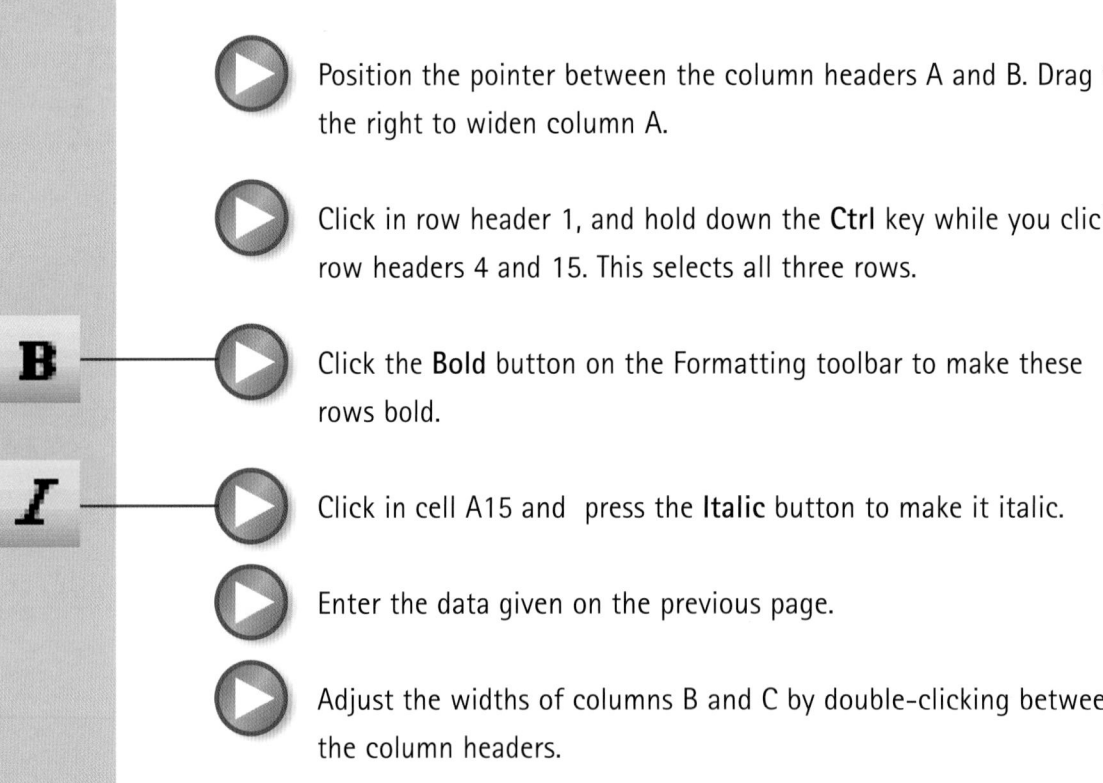

	A	B	C	D	E	F
1	Decline in songbird numbers between 1972 and 1996					
2	(Numbers given in millions)					
3						
4		1972	1996			
5	Skylark					
6	Willow warbler					
7	Linnet					
8	Song thrush					
9	Lapwing					
10	Yellowhammer					
11	Blackbird					
12	Tree sparrow					
13	Corn bunting					
14						
15	Source: British Trust for Ornithology					
16						

Figure 5.1

Position the pointer between the column headers A and B. Drag to the right to widen column A.

Click in row header 1, and hold down the **Ctrl** key while you click in row headers 4 and 15. This selects all three rows.

Click the **Bold** button on the Formatting toolbar to make these rows bold.

Click in cell A15 and press the **Italic** button to make it italic.

Enter the data given on the previous page.

Adjust the widths of columns B and C by double-clicking between the column headers.

When you have done that, your spreadsheet will look like this:

	A	B	C	D	E	
1	**Decline in songbird numbers between 1972 and 1996**					
2	(Numbers given in millions)					
3						
4		**1972**	**1996**			
5	Skylark	7.72	3.09			
6	Willow warbler	6.06	4.67			
7	Linnet	1.56	0.925			
8	Song thrush	3.62	1.74			
9	Lapwing	0.588	0.341			
10	Yellowhammer	4.4	1.76			
11	Blackbird	12.54	8.4			
12	Tree sparrow	0.65	0.0845			
13	Corn bunting	0.144	0.03			
14						
15	*Source: British Trust for Ornithology*					
16						

Figure 5.2

 Save your workbook, naming it **Birds.**

Drawing a bar chart

Now we can draw a bar chart to show this data.

 Click in A4 and drag diagonally through to C13 to select the cells to
be charted.

 Click the **Chart Wizard** button on the Standard toolbar. —————————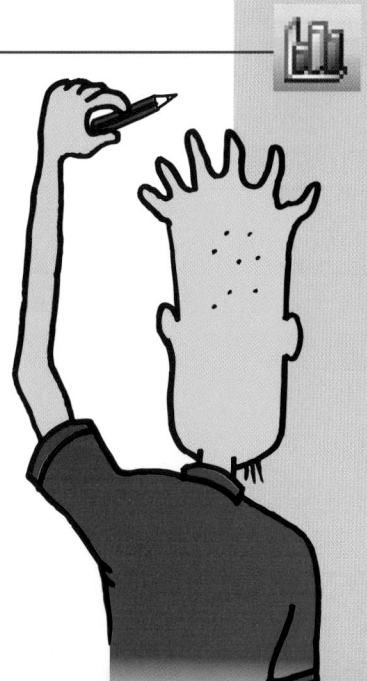

You will see a dialogue box something like the one shown below:

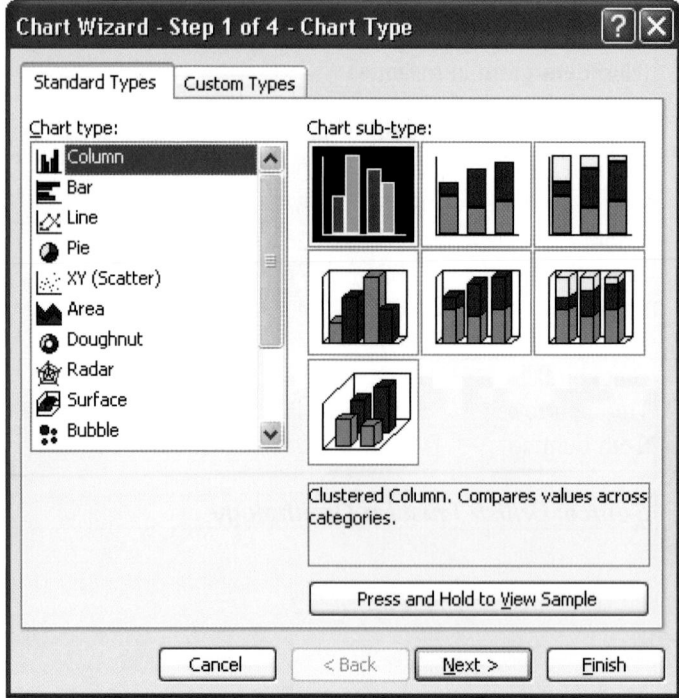

Figure 5.3

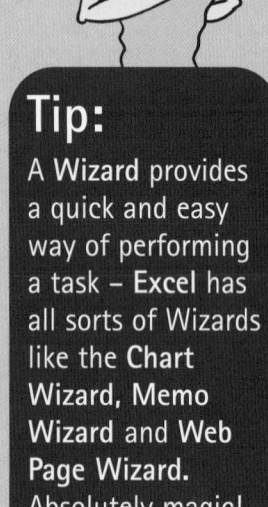

Tip:

A **Wizard** provides a quick and easy way of performing a task – **Excel** has all sorts of Wizards like the **Chart Wizard, Memo Wizard** and **Web Page Wizard.** Absolutely magic!

 Leave the first Chart sub-type selected.

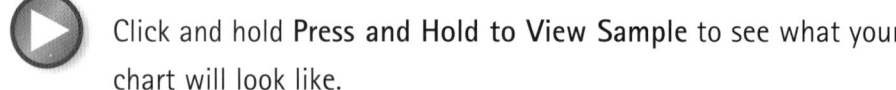 Click and hold **Press and Hold to View Sample** to see what your chart will look like.

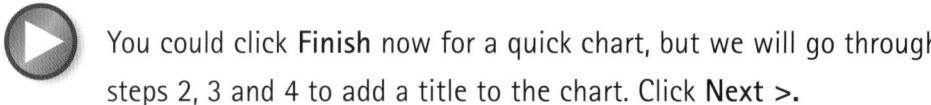 You could click **Finish** now for a quick chart, but we will go through steps 2, 3 and 4 to add a title to the chart. Click **Next >.**

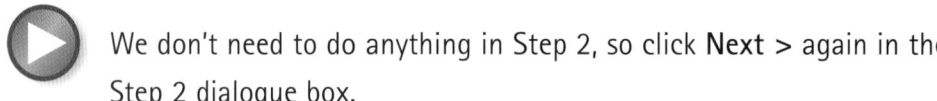 We don't need to do anything in Step 2, so click **Next >** again in the Step 2 dialogue box.

The Step 3 dialogue box appears.

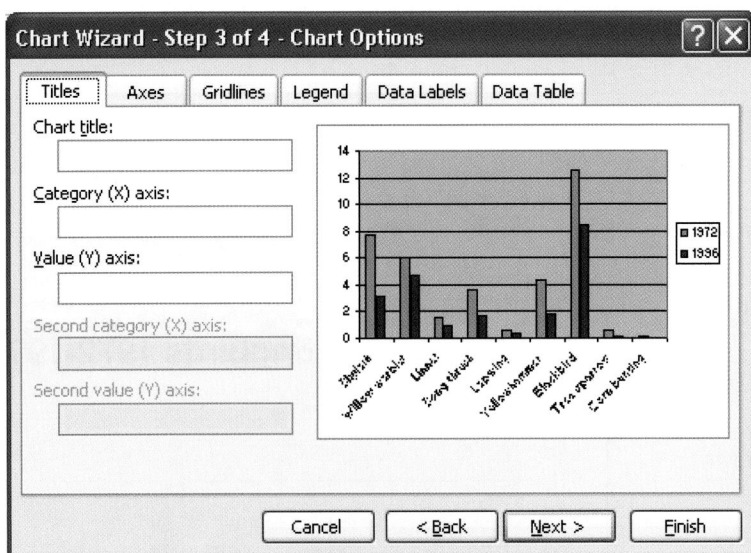

Figure 5.4

 In the Chart title box, type **Decline in songbirds 1972–1996** and then press **Next >.**

In the Step 4 dialogue box you can specify where you want the chart to appear. It can either be placed on its own in a new chart sheet, or it can be placed in the current sheet, **Sheet1.**

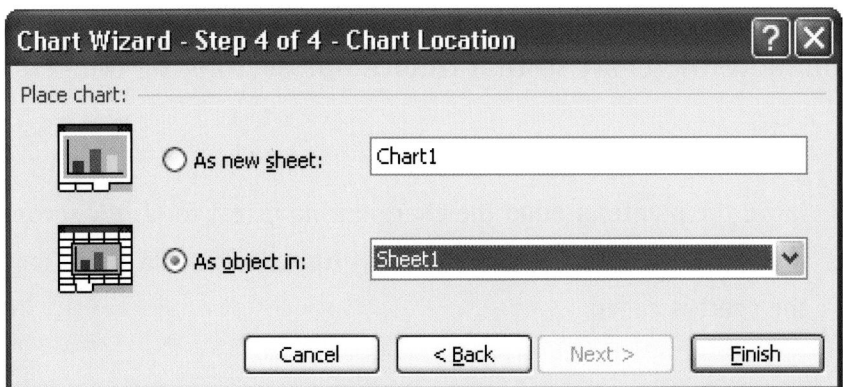

Figure 5.5

 Leave the default, **As Object in Sheet1.** Click **Finish.**

Your chart will appear something like the one shown below:

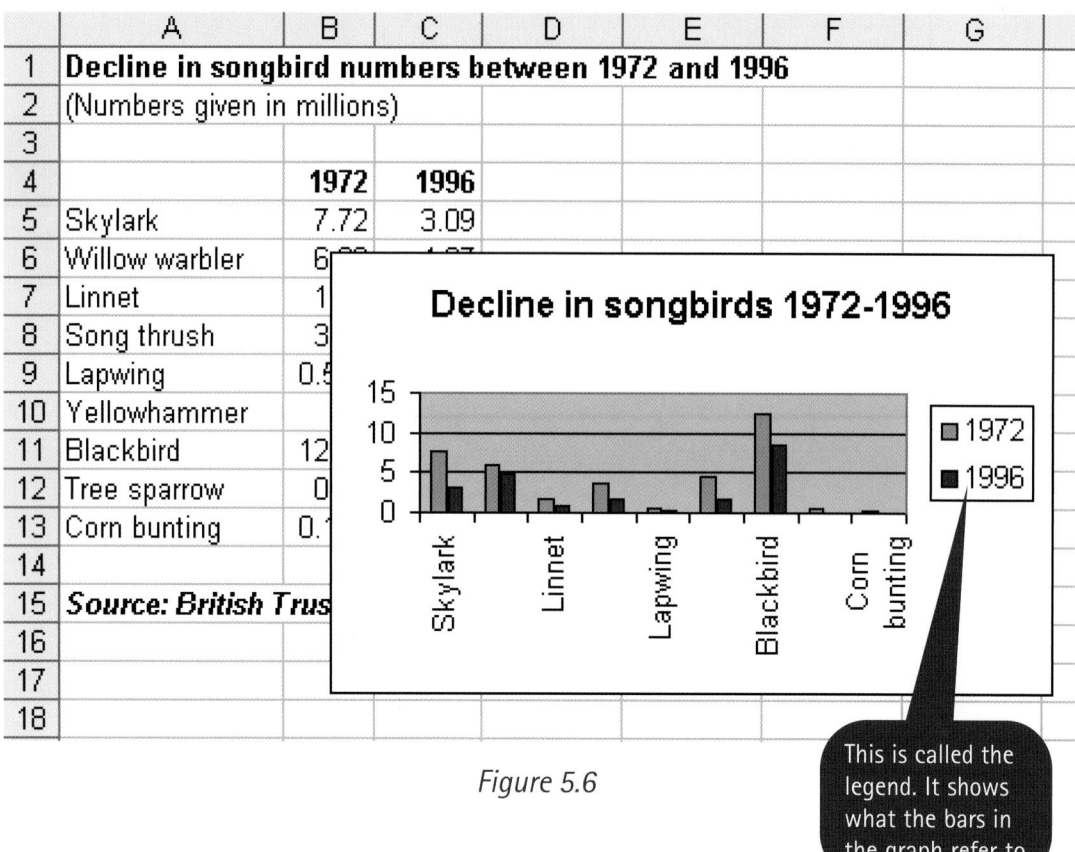

	A	B	C	D	E	F	G
1	**Decline in songbird numbers between 1972 and 1996**						
2	(Numbers given in millions)						
3							
4		**1972**	**1996**				
5	Skylark	7.72	3.09				
6	Willow warbler	6					
7	Linnet	1					
8	Song thrush	3					
9	Lapwing	0.5					
10	Yellowhammer						
11	Blackbird	12					
12	Tree sparrow	0					
13	Corn bunting	0.1					
14							
15	*Source: British Trus*						
16							
17							
18							

Figure 5.6

This is called the legend. It shows what the bars in the graph refer to.

Moving and sizing a chart

You can move the chart so that it does not overlap the data.

 Move the pointer around the chart, letting it rest for a few seconds in different places. Notice that a **tool tip** tells you what each part of the chart is called.

 See if you can identify parts of the chart called **chart area, plot area, legend, category axis, value axis, series "1972", series "1996".**

 Click in the **chart area** and drag the chart below the data.

 Drag the bottom right hand corner handle of the chart to make it bigger without distorting it.

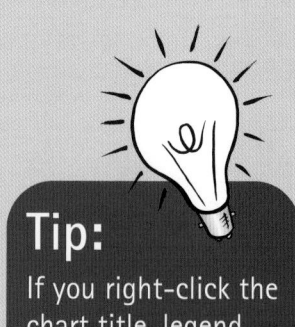

Tip:

If you right-click the chart title, legend or either axis, a shortcut menu will appear. Using the **Format** option you will be able to change the font.

Previewing and printing your chart

You may want to print your chart. You can print just the chart, or the chart together with the data.

First we'll see what the chart would look like printed on its own.

 Make sure the chart is selected. (It will have handles around it. Click in the **chart area** to select it if it is not already selected.)

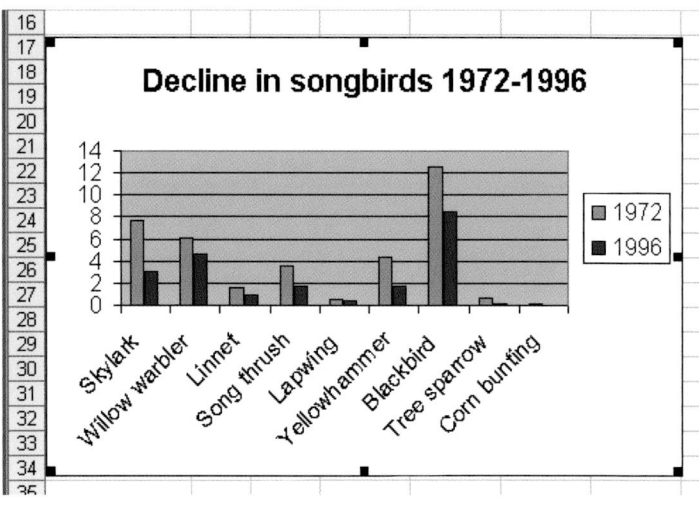

Figure 5.7

 Click the **Print Preview** button.

You may also want to format your chart. To change text orientation on the category axis, move the pointer over the axis and right-click. From the drop down menu select **Format Axis**. From the next screen select the **Alignment** tab and set the orientation degree.

You can also click the **Scale** tab and change the setting **Number of categories between tick-mark labels** from 2 to 1.

In a similar manner, you can change the scale on the y-axis. Move the pointer over the y-axis, right-click and choose **Format Axis**. With the **Scale** tab selected, and change the **Maximum** to 15 and **Major Unit** to 5.

Your chart should look something like Figure 5.7.

You will see on the screen how your chart will appear when it is printed.

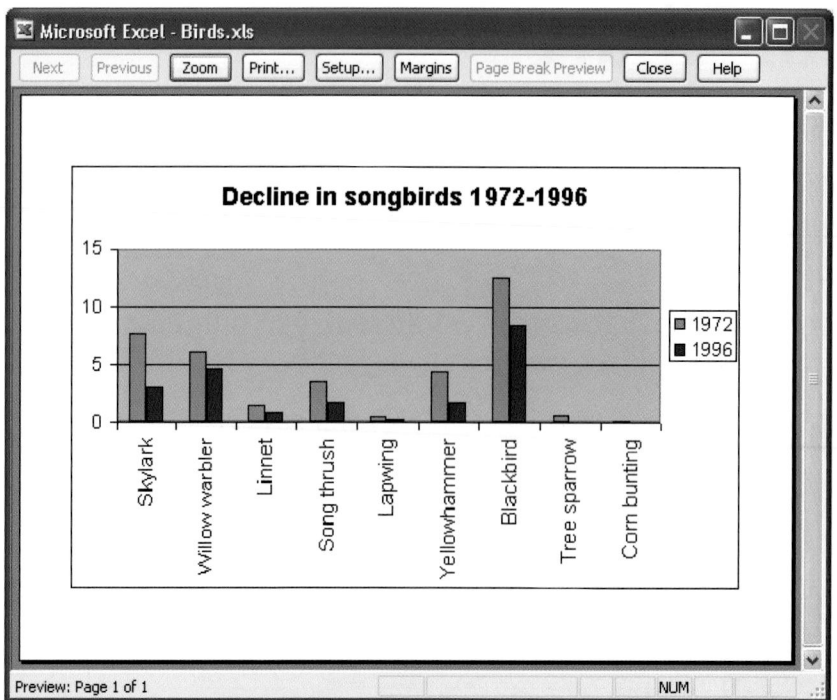

Figure 5.8

 If your computer is connected to a printer and you have permission to print, click the **Print** button at the top of the screen.

You will see the Print dialogue box:

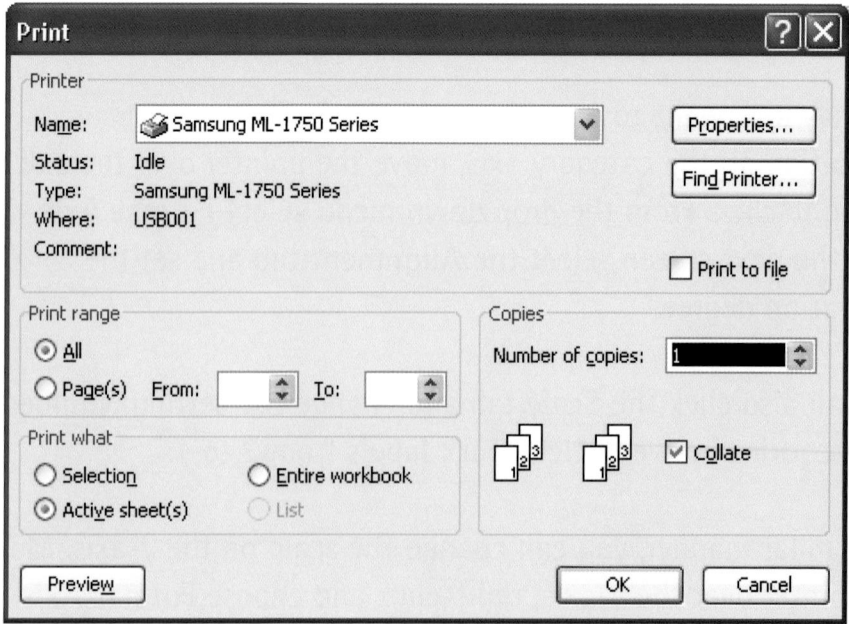

Figure 5.9

 Click **OK**.

 To print the data and the chart together, click away from the chart. Then press the **Print Preview** button. Your preview will look something like this:

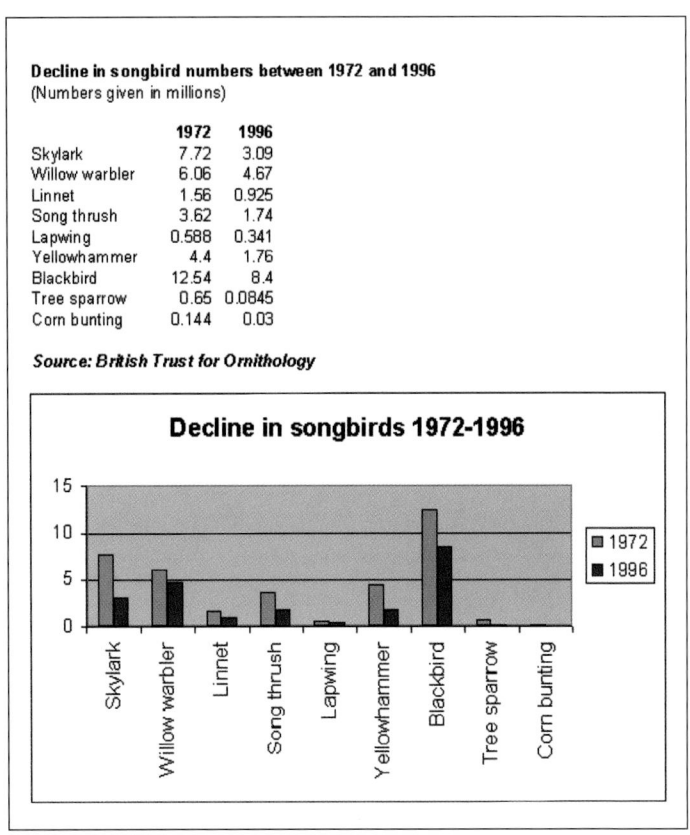

Decline in songbird numbers between 1972 and 1996
(Numbers given in millions)

	1972	1996
Skylark	7.72	3.09
Willow warbler	6.06	4.67
Linnet	1.56	0.925
Song thrush	3.62	1.74
Lapwing	0.588	0.341
Yellowhammer	4.4	1.76
Blackbird	12.54	8.4
Tree sparrow	0.65	0.0845
Corn bunting	0.144	0.03

Source: British Trust for Ornithology

Figure 5.10

When you move the pointer over the page, it changes to a magnifying glass. Click it to zoom in on the page. Now take a look at your chart and see what it tells you.

Additional exercise

Dave and Doreen Thurber are planning a holiday in Sicily.
They want to go when the weather is not too hot or cold,
and the travel brochure gives the average maximum monthly
temperatures as follows:

Month	Average maximum temperature (°C)	Average minimum temperature (°C)
Jan	11	4
Feb	13	5
Mar	16	6
Apr	18	8
May	23	12
June	27	16
Jul	31	18
Aug	29	18
Sep	27	16
Oct	23	13
Nov	17	8
Dec	12	5

Design a worksheet for these measurements.

Show each set of figures on a bar chart or a line graph.

Which months would be best for Dave and Doreen Thurber to go
on holiday?

Chapter 6
Pie Charts

You've tried a bar chart – now how about a pie chart? We'll use the same spreadsheet that you created in the last chapter.

 Open the workbook **Birds** created in the last chapter.

We'll draw a pie chart showing the numbers of different kinds of songbirds (in millions) in the UK in 1996.

 Drag across cells A5 to A13 to select them.

 Hold down the **Ctrl** key while you select cells C5 to C13.

	A	B	C	D	E	F	G	H
1	**Decline in songbird numbers between 1972 and 1996**							
2	(Numbers given in millions)							
3								
4		**1972**	**1996**					
5	Skylark	7.72	3.09					
6	Willow warbler	6.06	4.67					
7	Linnet	1.56	0.925					
8	Song thrush	3.62	1.74					
9	Lapwing	0.588	0.341					
10	Yellowhammer	4.4	1.76					
11	Blackbird	12.54	8.4					
12	Tree sparrow	0.65	0.0845					
13	Corn bunting	0.144	0.03					
14								
15	*Source: British Trust for Ornithology*							
16								
17								

Birds.xls — Sheet1 / Sheet2 / Sheet3

Figure 6.1

 Click the **Chart Wizard** button on the Standard toolbar.

In the dialogue box, select **Pie** in the Chart type list box.

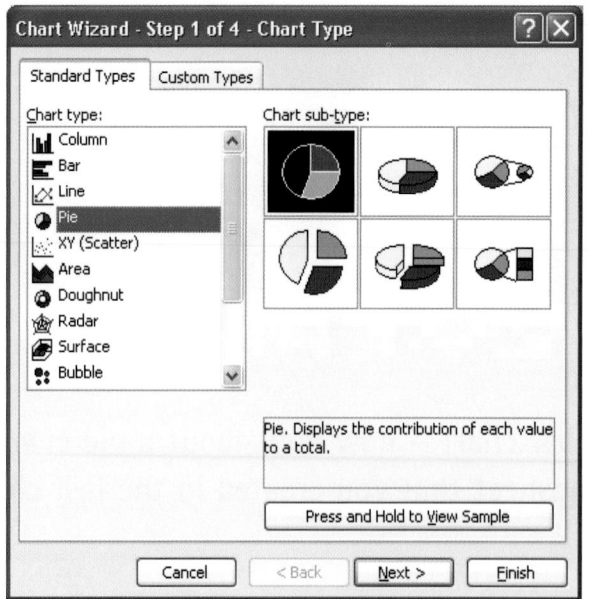

Figure 6.2

 Leave the first option selected for Chart sub-type and click **Next.**

 Click **Next** in the Step 2 dialogue box.

 Make sure the **Titles** tab is selected. Type the title **Songbirds 1996.**

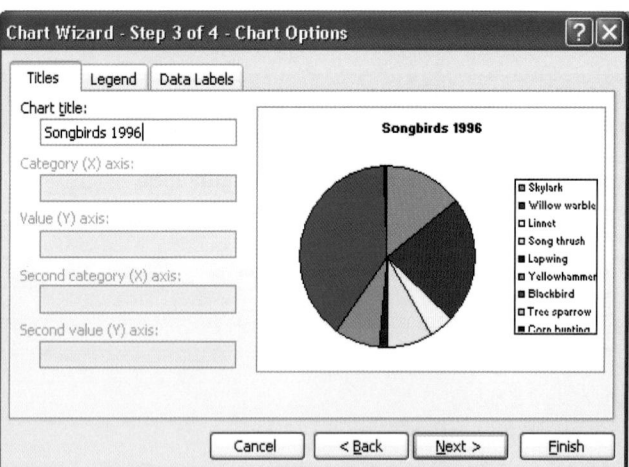

Figure 6.3

 Click the **Legend** tab just to see what the options are.

 You can experiment to see where you want to put the legend. In Figure 6.4 **Right** has been selected.

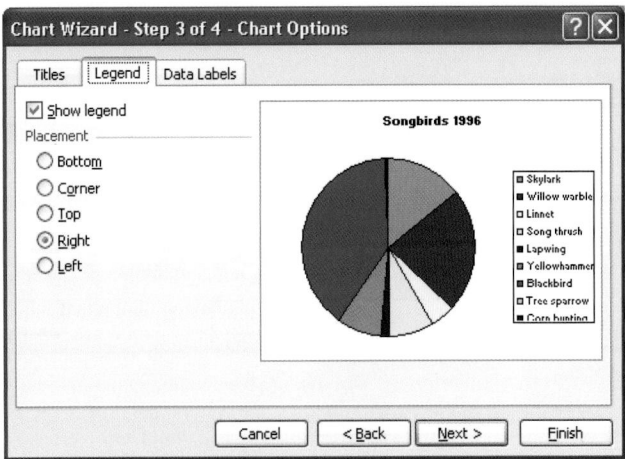

Figure 6.4

 Click the **Data Labels** tab.

At the moment Data Labels is set to **None.**

 Click **Percentage** and **Category name**.

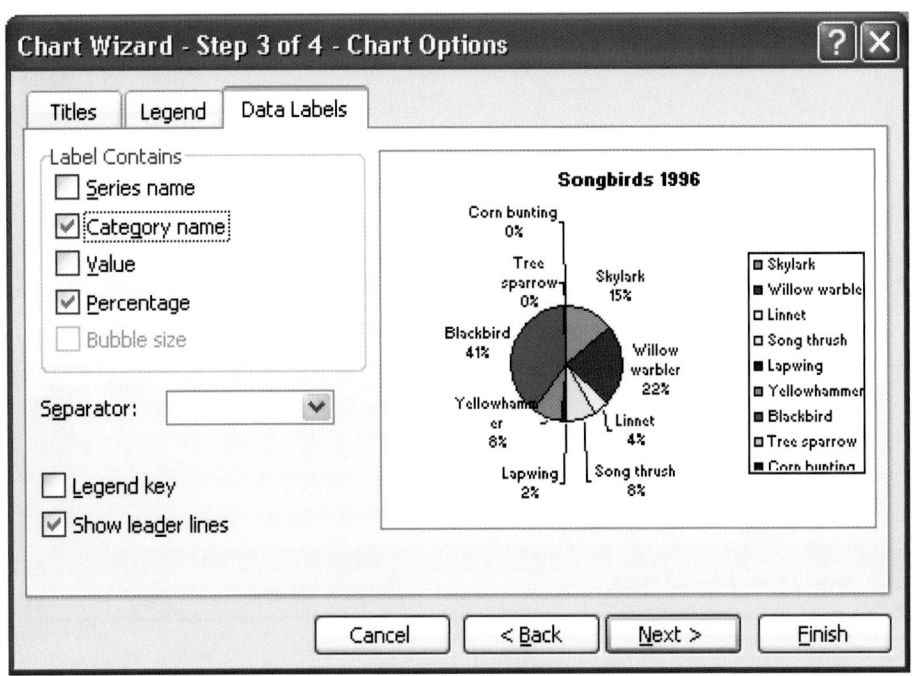

Figure 6.5

 Click **Next.**

 This time we will place the chart in a separate Chart sheet.
Click **As new sheet.**

Tip:
The **Legend** is the key to what colour represents which bird.

Note:
In Excel 2000 click **Show Label and percent**.

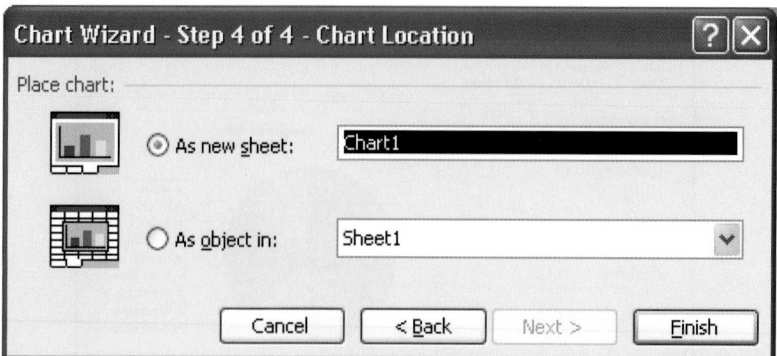

Figure 6.6

 Click **Finish.**

The chart appears in a new Chart Sheet.

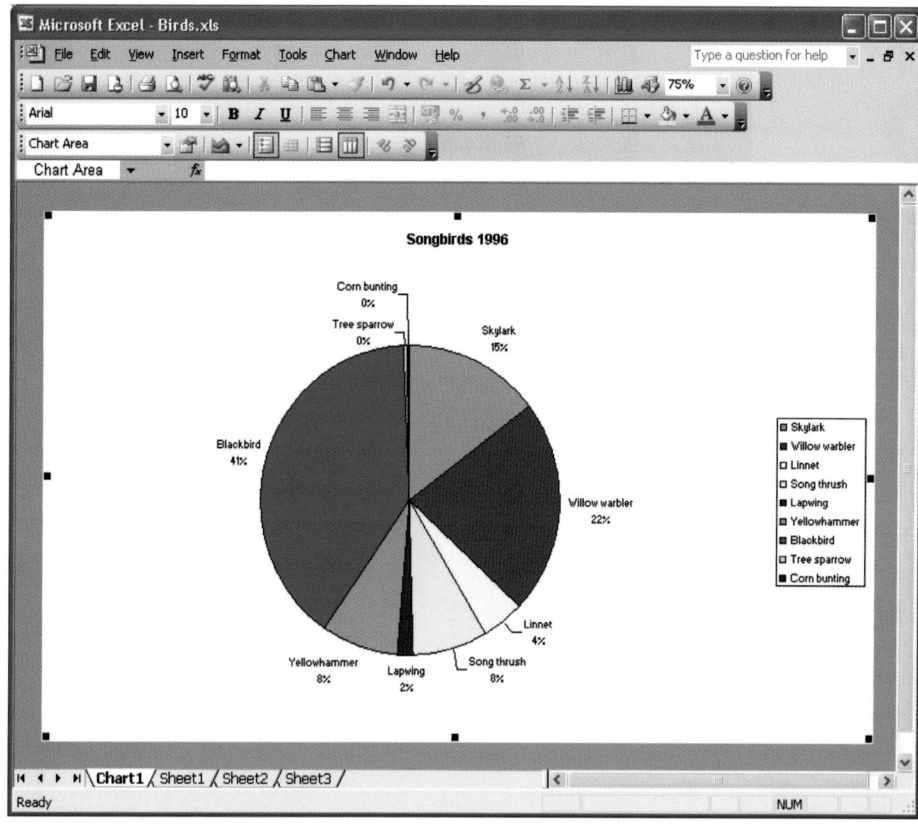

Figure 6.7

Formatting the data labels

The labels are rather small. Also, the percentages are shown only as whole numbers and we would like them displayed to 2 decimal places.

 Right-click any of the data labels.

 A shortcut menu appears. Click **Format Data Labels**.

 Click the **Font** tab in the dialogue box.

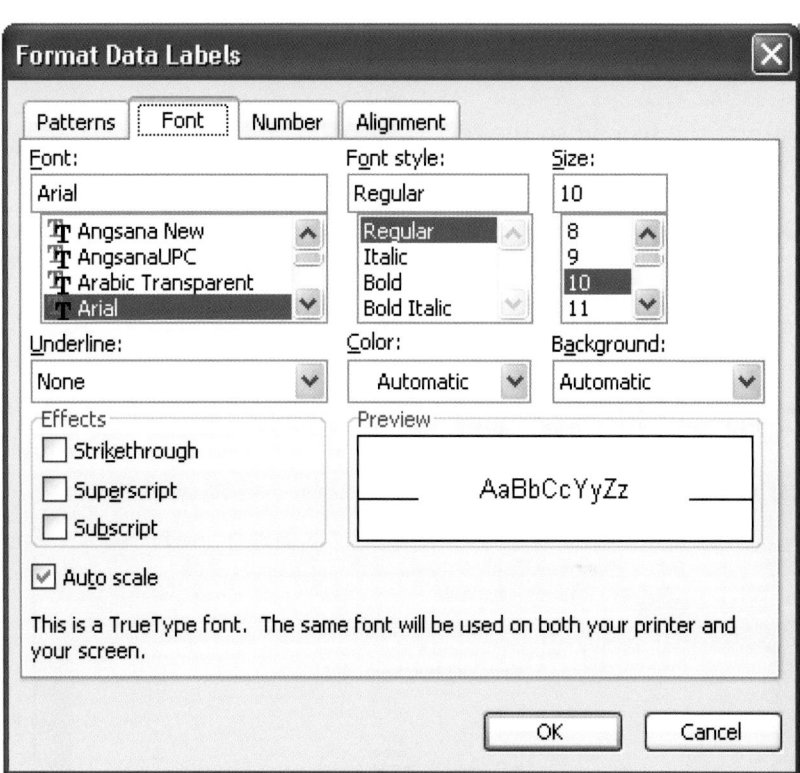

Figure 6.8

 Change the font size to **12.**

 Click the **Number** tab.

 Click **Percentage** in the Category list box if it is not already selected.

 Enter **2** as the number of Decimal places.

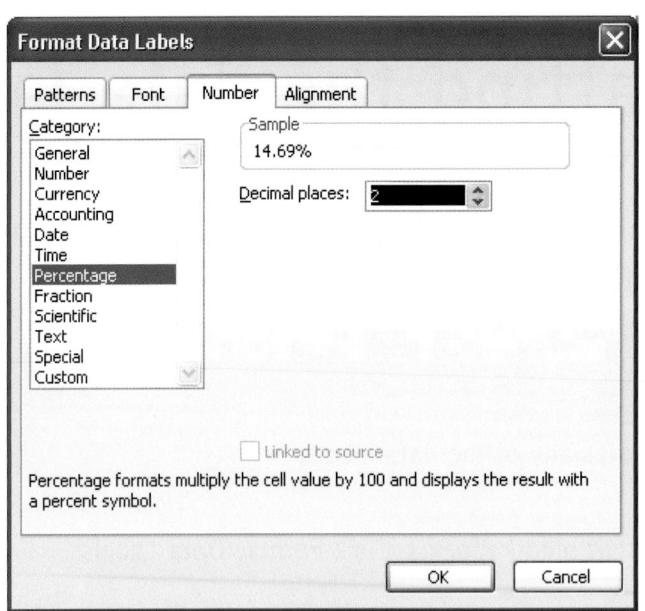

Figure 6.9

Tip:

To change the text of the **Chart Title,** click it to select it and then click in the text where you want to insert or delete text.

Click **OK.**

Format the **legend** so the text is 12 point.

Drag the legend a little closer to the pie chart.

Format the **Chart Title** to 18 point.

Change the title to **Songbird Numbers 1996.**

Click here to return to Sheet1, where you typed the data

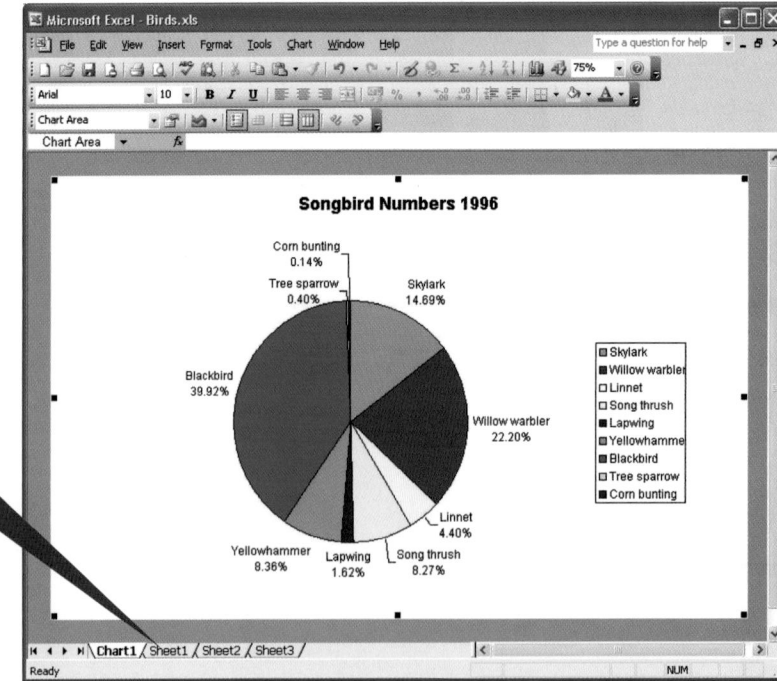

Figure 6.10

Tip:

Click **Print Preview**

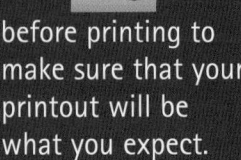

before printing to make sure that your printout will be what you expect.

Save your workbook.

If your computer is connected to a printer, you may like to print it.

Chapter 7
Creating a Form

In this chapter you are going to carry on with the survey of classmates that was started in Chapter 3.

The new survey will find out how many different fruits and vegetables are eaten daily by pupils in a group.

Data will be collected over a period of a week and recorded by hand in a worksheet created for this purpose. Once the data has been collected, it can be entered into the computer, statistics calculated, and conclusions drawn.

> Nutritionists recommend that we all eat at least 5 or 6 different types of fruit or vegetable every day – better still, eat 9 or 10! Crisps and strawberry jam don't count, by the way.

Project: Create a form for data collection.

 Open the worksheet **Stats** created in Chapters 3 and 4.

It should look similar to the one below.

	A	B	C	D	E	F
1	MEASUREMENTS		CLASS 6R		Name:	Frances Lake
2						
3	Name	Height(cm)	Weight(kg)	Foot length(cm)		
4	Anthony Goddard	131.5	35.3	19.5		
5	Timothy Salter	126.0	30.0	18.4		
6	Kerry Meredith	138.0	39.5	21.0		
7	Deborah Roberts	129.7	34.8	18.3		
8	Hussen Shah	132.5	33.0	20.3		
9	Touqir Mylas	130.0	34.0	19.0		
10	Jacob Walton	139.0	40.0	22.5		
11						
12	TOTAL	926.7	246.6	139.0		
13						
14	AVERAGE	132.4	35.2	19.9		
15						
16	MAXIMUM	139.0	40.0	22.5		
17						
18	MINIMUM	126.0	30.0	18.3		
19						

Sheet tabs

Sheet1 / Sheet2 / Sheet3 /

Figure 7.1

Naming worksheets

The workbook shown above contains 3 worksheets called **Sheet1, Sheet2,** and **Sheet3.**

Look at the sheet tabs at the bottom of the screenshot. **Sheet1** is the active sheet. We will rename **Sheet1** to give it a more meaningful name. We'll be using **Sheet2** for the new survey so we'll rename that too.

▶ Right-click the **Sheet1** tab.

▶ Select **Rename** from the shortcut menu. **Excel** highlights the name **Sheet1.**

▶ Type the new name Measurements.

▶ Press **Enter.**

▶ Now rename **Sheet2,** giving it the name **Fruit and Veg.** Remember to press **Enter** after typing the new name.

▶ Type the new heading Healthy Eating Survey in cell A1 of the **Fruit and Veg** worksheet.

B ▶ Click the row selector for Row 1 and click the **Bold** button on the Formatting toolbar to make all entries in this row bold.

Copying data between sheets

We can copy some of the headings and names from the **Measurements** sheet instead of typing them all again.

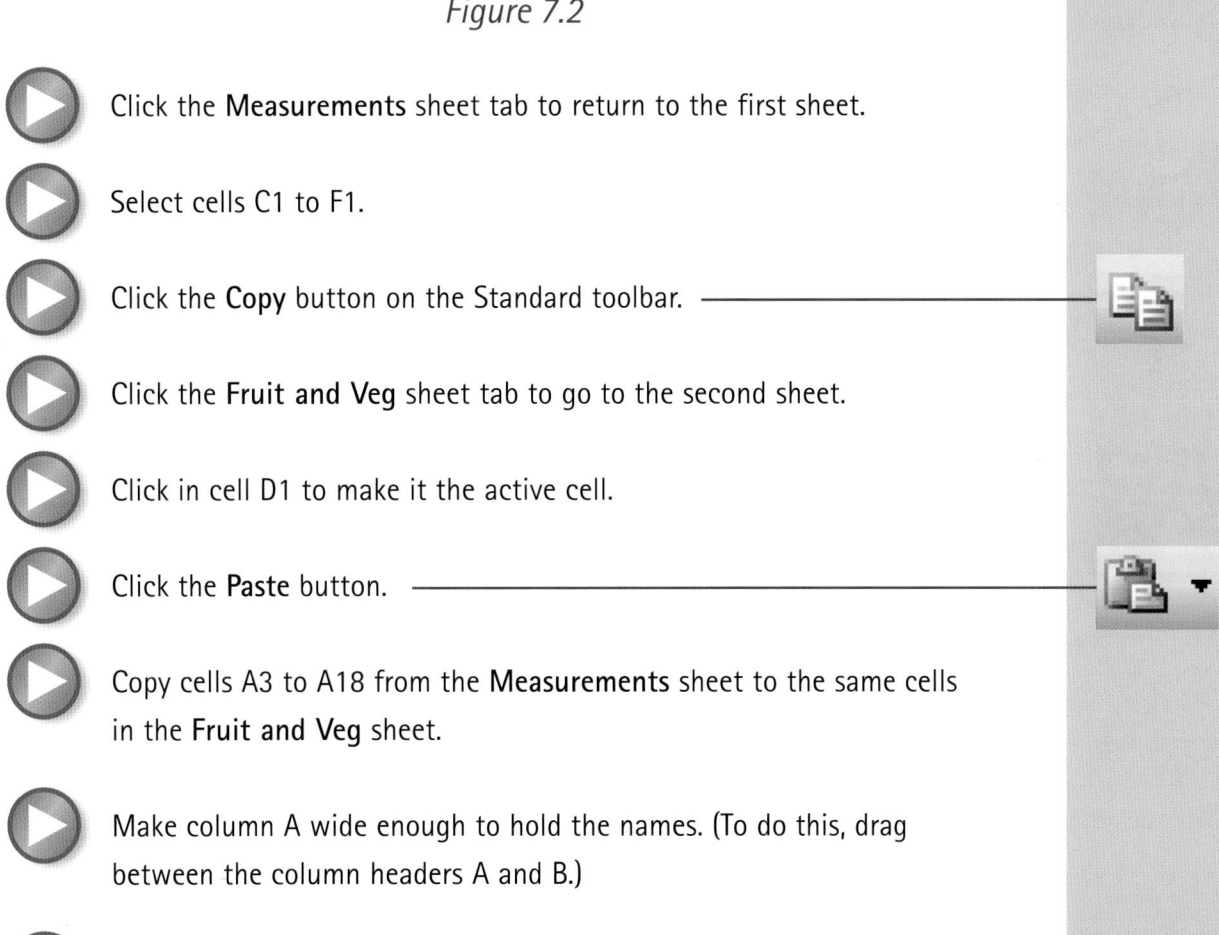

Figure 7.2

Click the **Measurements** sheet tab to return to the first sheet.

Select cells C1 to F1.

Click the **Copy** button on the Standard toolbar. ───────────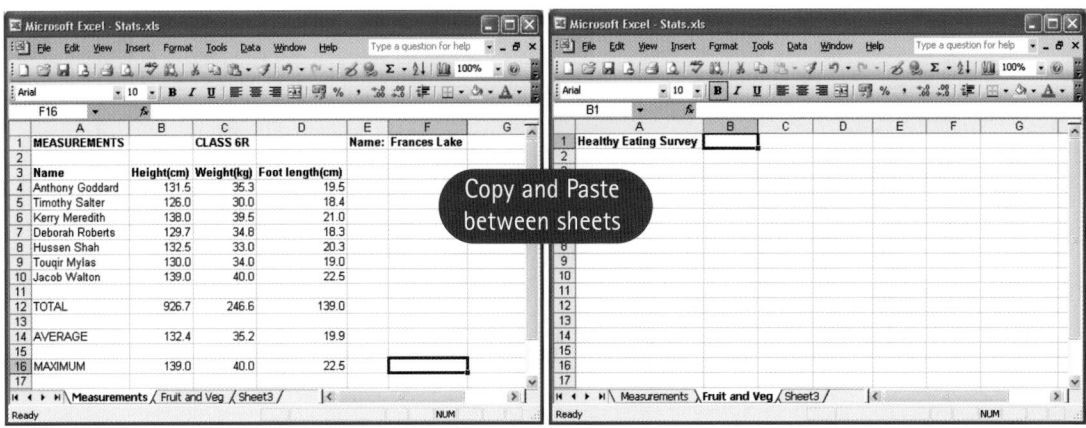

Click the **Fruit and Veg** sheet tab to go to the second sheet.

Click in cell D1 to make it the active cell.

Click the **Paste** button. ───────────

Copy cells A3 to A18 from the **Measurements** sheet to the same cells in the **Fruit and Veg** sheet.

Make column A wide enough to hold the names. (To do this, drag between the column headers A and B.)

In cell B3, type **Monday.**

Click in row header 3 to select the row. Use the **Bold** button to make all the cells bold. (You may have to press it twice.)

Now your worksheet should look similar to the one below:

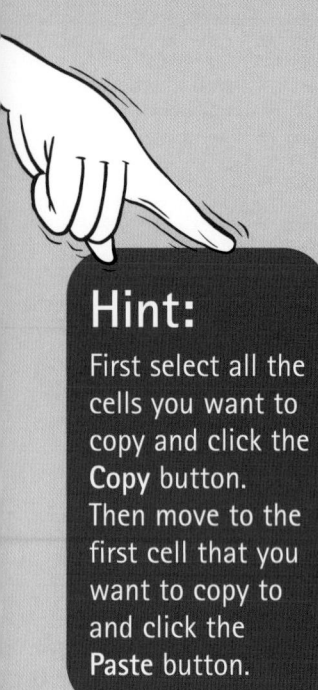

	A	B	C	D	E	F	G
	B3		fx	Monday			
1	Healthy Eating Survey			CLASS 6R		Name:	Frances Lake
2							
3	Name	Monday					
4	Anthony Goddard						
5	Timothy Salter						
6	Kerry Meredith						
7	Deborah Roberts						
8	Hussen Shah						
9	Touqir Mylas						
10	Jacob Walton						
11							
12	TOTAL						
13							
14	AVERAGE						
15							
16	MAXIMUM						
17							
18	MINIMUM						

Measurements \ **Fruit and Veg** \ Sheet3 /

Figure 7.3

Hint:

First select all the cells you want to copy and click the **Copy** button. Then move to the first cell that you want to copy to and click the **Paste** button.

Filling a series

Instead of typing all the other days of the week in cells C3 to F3, you can let **Excel** do it for you.

 Click cell B3.

 Click and drag the little square in the bottom right hand corner of the cell. This is called the **Fill handle.** Drag it to cell F3.

Tip:

You can copy formulae using the Fill handle too. Make sure the mouse pointer looks like a cross, not an arrow, when you do this.

	A	B	C	D	E	F
1	Healthy Eating Survey			CLASS 6R		Name: Fran(
2						
3	Name	Monday				
4	Anthony Goddard					Friday
5	Timothy Salter					

Figure 7.4

Click and drag this handle to cell F3

Now your headings should look like this:

	A	B	C	D	E	F	G
1	Healthy Eating Survey			CLASS 6R		Name:	Frances Lake
2							
3	Name	Monday	Tuesday	Wednesda	Thursday	Friday	
4	Anthony Goddard						
5	Timothy Salter						

Figure 7.5

 Double-click between column headers D and E to widen column D.

Increasing the row height

As this worksheet is to be used as a data entry form which will be filled in by hand, there needs to be more space between rows.

 Drag across row headers 4 - 10 to select these rows.

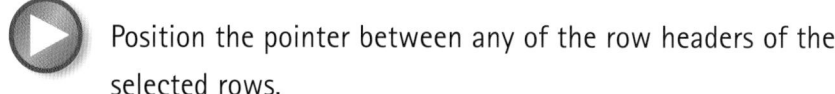 Position the pointer between any of the row headers of the selected rows.

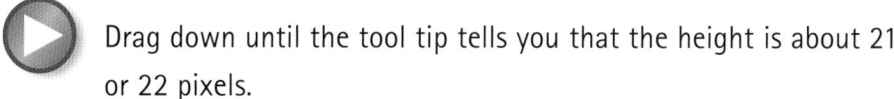 Drag down until the tool tip tells you that the height is about 21 or 22 pixels.

Drag between any of the row headers to increase the row height of the selected rows.

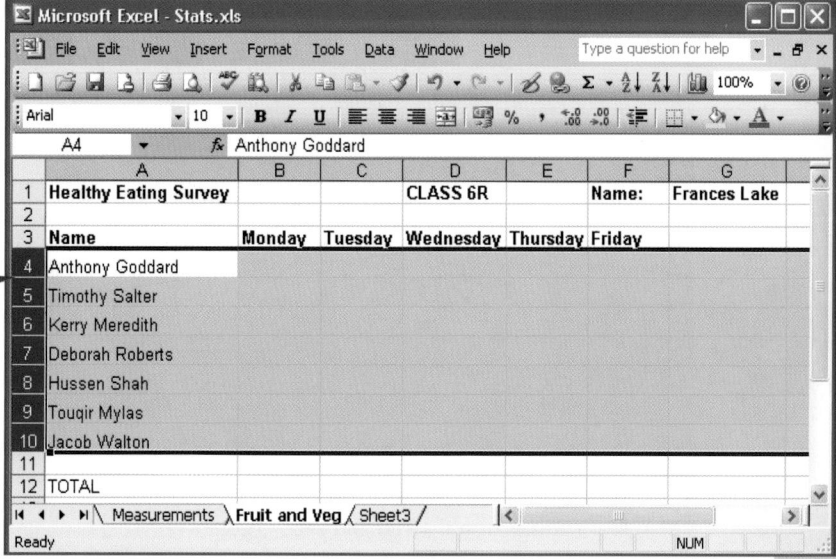

Figure 7.6

Adding cell borders

 Press the **Print Preview** button.

The form is not really suitable for filling in data by hand. It needs borders around each cell so that you can see which column and row you are in.

 Press the **Esc** key to leave **Print Preview** mode.

 Select cells A3 to F10.

 Click the down arrow next to the **Borders** button.

 Select the border shown below.

Tip:

Esc is at the top left of the keyboard. It's a very useful key when you can't think of anything else to press.

Tip:

If your version does not have the Border icon, select **Format, Cells** from the menu. Click the **Border** tab and click the **Outline** and **Inside** borders.

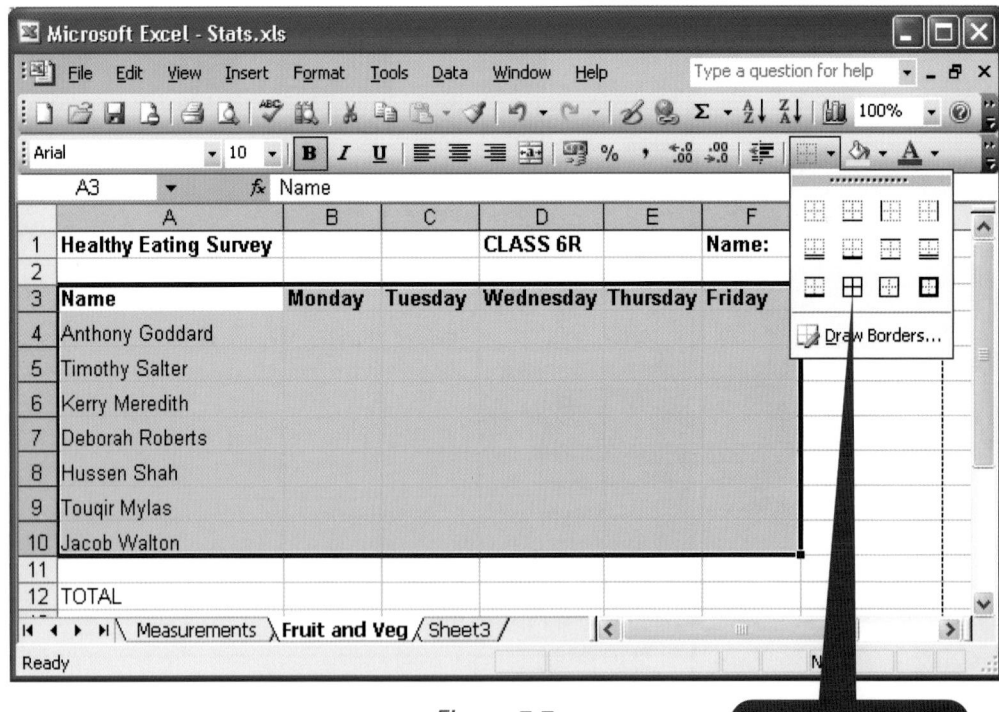

Figure 7.7

Select this border

Merging and centering cells

We will add a heading which will be centred across the top row.

 Select Row headers 1 and 2. Click the right mouse button to display the shortcut menu.

 Select **Insert** from the shortcut menu to add 2 new rows at the top of the page.

 Type **Data Entry Form** in cell A1 and press **Enter.**

 Select cells A1 to F1 by dragging across them.

 Click the **Merge and Center** button on the Formatting toolbar.

This makes cells A1 to F1 into a single cell referred to as A1.

 Make the heading in cell A1 Bold, size 18 point. You may need to increase the row height so that the text fits in the row.

	A	B	C	D	E	F	G
1				Data Entry Form			
2							
3	Healthy Eating Survey			CLASS 6R		Name:	Frances Lake
4							
5	Name	Monday	Tuesday	Wednesday	Thursday	Friday	
6	Anthony Goddard						

Figure 7.8

Aligning text and numbers

It's advisable to leave the numbers right-aligned in the cells. The headings **Monday, Tuesday** etc look better right-aligned too.

 Select cells B5 to F5.

 Click the **Align Right** button.

Setting the print area

For the data entry form you don't really need the labels Total, Average, Maximum and Minimum at the bottom of the form. You can choose to print only part of the worksheet.

 Select cells A1 to H12.

 From the main menu select **File.** Then select **Print Area, Set Print Area.**

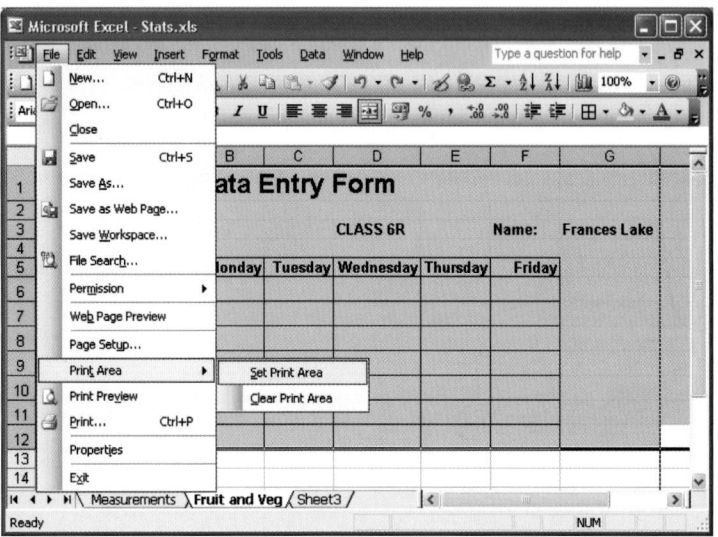

Figure 7.9

 Press **Print Preview** again. The name may not quite fit on the page.

 Press the **Setup..** button at the top of the screen. You will see the following window:

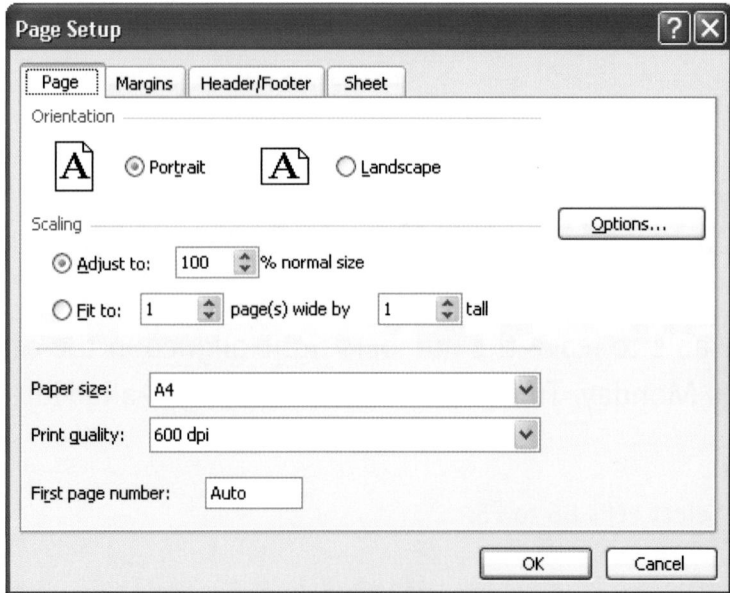

Figure 7.10

Click the **Fit to:** radio button to make all the text fit on a single page. Then click **OK.**

 Click anywhere on the page where the pointer appears as a magnifying glass to see the preview in more detail.

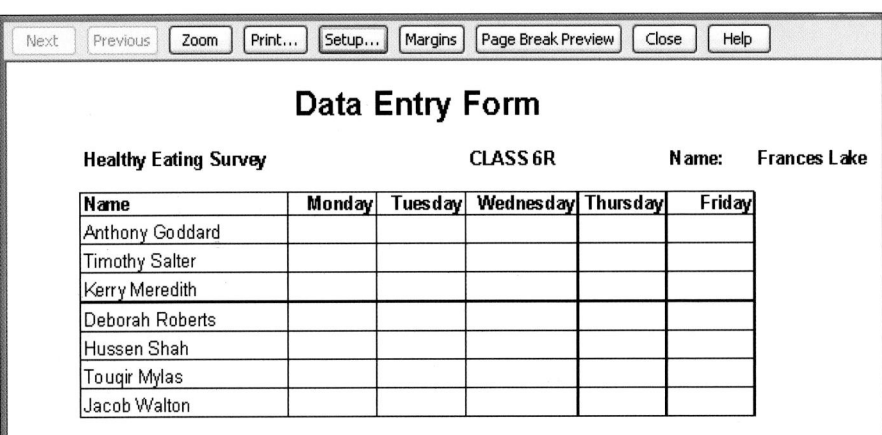

Figure 7.11

Make sure your own name is on the form before you print. You can return to Normal view by pressing **Esc** or the **Close** button.

From Print Preview, press **Print...** to print your form.

Save your workbook.

Additional exercise

On **Sheet3** of this workbook create a data entry form for a survey of who was born in which month.

Name the sheet **Birthdays.**

Your form could look something like the one below.

Zoom button

A	B	C	D	E	F	G	H	I	J	K	L
					Survey of Birthday Months						
January	February	March	April	May	June	July	August	September	October	November	December

Figure 7.12

▶ Type the heading **Survey of Birthday Months** in cell A1. Merge and centre it by selecting cells A1 to L1 and then clicking the **Merge and Center** button.

▶ Once you have typed the heading **January,** you can drag the Fill handle to fill in all the other months automatically.

▶ You can use the **Zoom** button to view the worksheet at 90% of full size so that it fits on the screen. Type **90** in the 100% box and press **Enter.**

▶ It will have to be printed in Landscape view. From the **File** menu choose **Page Setup** and click **Landscape** in the dialogue box. Then click **OK.**

▶ Click **Print Preview** before you print your worksheet to make sure it looks OK. Press **Print...** to print the form when you are satisfied it is correct.

Then you can carry out your survey! The results could be plotted on a bar chart.

Tip:

In **Landscape** setting the page is printed sideways. In **Portrait** setting the page is printed lengthways like a page in this book.

Chapter 8
Moving and Copying

A week has passed, and the data on Healthy Eating has been collected. Now it's time to enter the data and find out just how healthy or unhealthy your classmates' diet is.

Along the way you'll learn more about moving and copying data, and formatting text and numbers.

Here is the data entry form as completed by Frances Lake.

Healthy Eating Survey   CLASS 6R   Name: Frances Lake

Name	Monday	Tuesday	Wednesday	Thursday	Friday
Anthony Goddard	4	4	7	3	4
Timothy Salter	6	9	10	5	9
Kerry Meredith	2	1	2	3	1
Deborah Roberts	5	5	6	5	3
Hussen Shah	4	4	3	5	6
Touqir Mylas	7	3	8	4	2
Jacob Walton	5	12	12	6	8

Figure 8.1

(Jacob's father made a huge fruit salad on Tuesday which the whole family had to eat again on Wednesday for breakfast.)

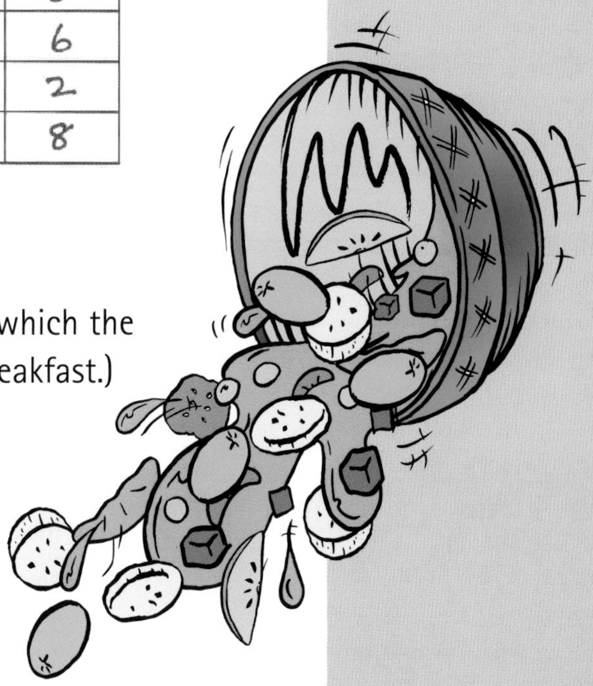

▶ Open the workbook **Stats** which you saved in the last chapter.

▶ Make sure the **Fruit and Veg** worksheet tab is selected.

▶ Enter all the data as shown in Figure 8.1.

Copying formulae from another sheet

You have already entered formulae for Total, Average, Maximum and Minimum in the **Measurements** worksheet. We can copy the formulae to the current worksheet.

▶ Click the **Measurements** worksheet tab.

▶ Select cells B12 to B18.

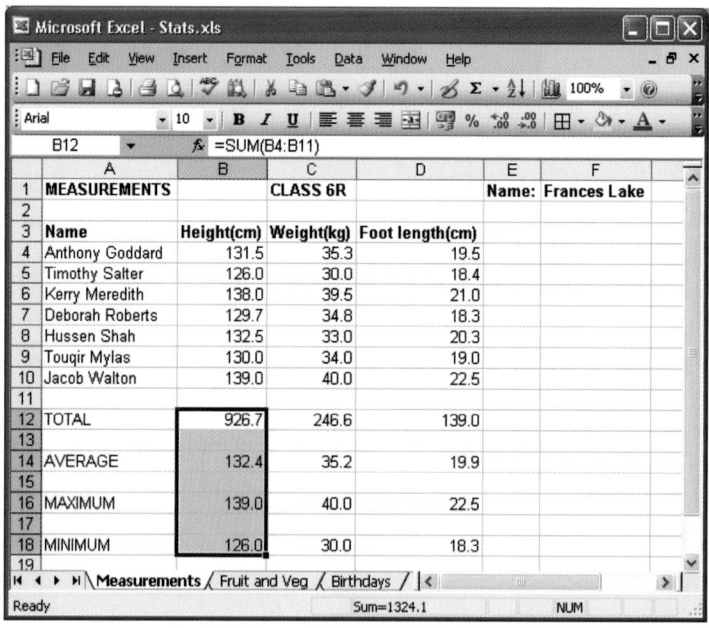

Figure 8.2

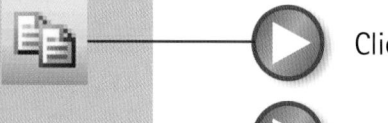

▶ Click the **Copy** button.

▶ Click the **Fruit and Veg** sheet tab.

▶ Click in cell B14 in the **Fruit and Veg** sheet.

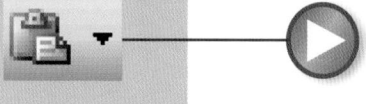

▶ Click the **Paste** button and notice the new values. Leave cells B14 to B20 selected after pasting them.

Copying using the Fill handle

In the last chapter you used the Fill handle to fill in the days of the week Tuesday to Saturday.

It is also used to quickly copy text, numbers and formulae to adjacent cells, instead of using the **Copy** and **Paste** buttons.

 Make sure cells B14 to B20 are selected.

 Drag the Fill handle from the bottom right-hand corner of cell B20 across to cell F20.

If it all goes horribly wrong click the **Undo** button and try again. The pointer should be a cross, not an arrow, when you drag the Fill handle.

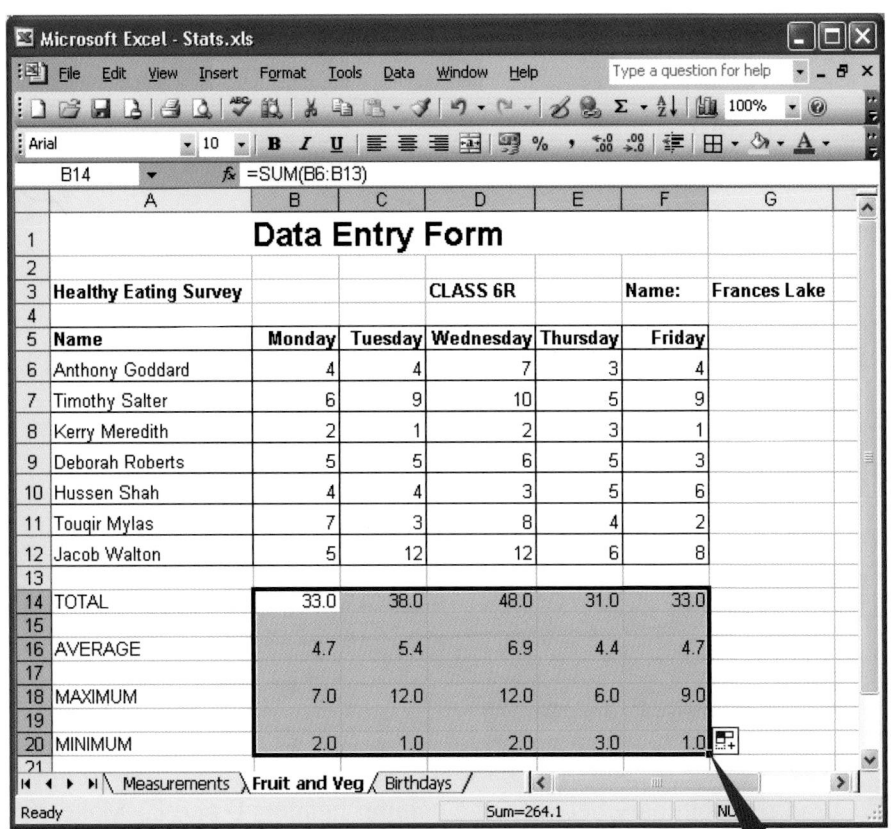

Figure 8.3

Drag the Fill handle to copy the cells

Check:

Do the figures for Total, Average, Maximum and Minimum look reasonable? Did anyone eat 48 different fruits and vegetables last Wednesday? I don't think so!

59

Moving cell contents

Let's move some cells in Row 3.

 Click cell D3.

 Drag its left hand border to cell C3.

 Select F3 and G3. Drag the left-hand border of F3 to cell E3 to move **Name: Frances Lake.**

Using the shortcut menu to copy and paste

As part of the data analysis we would like to know the average number of fruit and vegetables eaten by each member of the class.

We will copy the label **Average** from cell A16 to G5.

 Right-click cell A16.

 Select **Copy.**

 Right-click cell G5.

 Select **Paste.**

 Make the heading **AVERAGE** bold and right-align it.

You may need to widen the columns a little, and put a border around the cells in column G.

 Select column headers B to G.

 Drag the boundary between the column headers D and E. Make them wide enough to hold the longest heading, **Wednesday.**

 Use the **Borders** tool to put borders around the cells in column G.

Tip:
If you need help drawing borders, look back at Figure 7.7 in the last chapter.

Entering the formula for Average

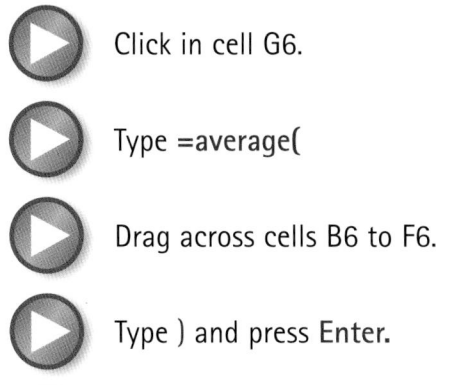

Click in cell G6.

Type =average(

Drag across cells B6 to F6.

Type) and press Enter.

Click in cell G6 and drag the Fill handle down to cell G12 to copy the formula to the other cells.

Copy the formula from F18 to G18, and from F20 to G20.

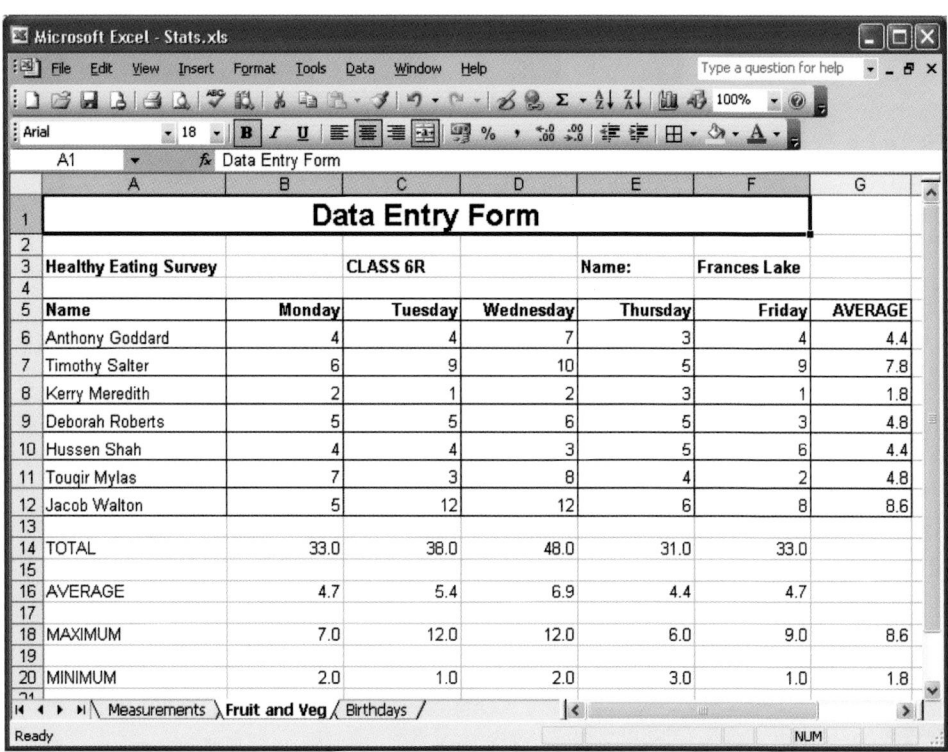

	A	B	C	D	E	F	G
1			Data Entry Form				
2							
3	Healthy Eating Survey		CLASS 6R		Name:	Frances Lake	
4							
5	Name	Monday	Tuesday	Wednesday	Thursday	Friday	AVERAGE
6	Anthony Goddard	4	4	7	3	4	4.4
7	Timothy Salter	6	9	10	5	9	7.8
8	Kerry Meredith	2	1	2	3	1	1.8
9	Deborah Roberts	5	5	6	5	3	4.8
10	Hussen Shah	4	4	3	5	6	4.4
11	Touqir Mylas	7	3	8	4	2	4.8
12	Jacob Walton	5	12	12	6	8	8.6
13							
14	TOTAL	33.0	38.0	48.0	31.0	33.0	
15							
16	AVERAGE	4.7	5.4	6.9	4.4	4.7	
17							
18	MAXIMUM	7.0	12.0	12.0	6.0	9.0	8.6
19							
20	MINIMUM	2.0	1.0	2.0	3.0	1.0	1.8

Figure 8.4

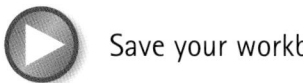

Save your workbook.

Printing the results

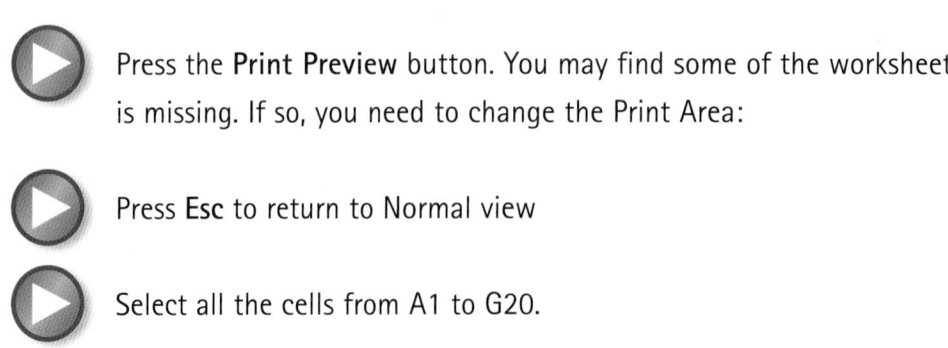 Press the **Print Preview** button. You may find some of the worksheet is missing. If so, you need to change the Print Area:

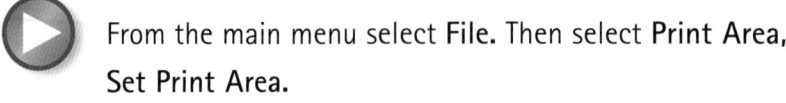 Press **Esc** to return to Normal view

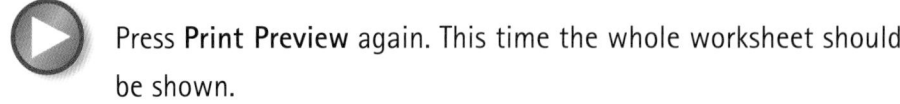 Select all the cells from A1 to G20.

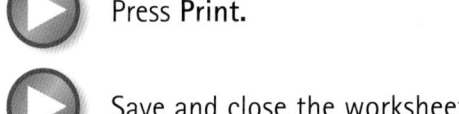 From the main menu select **File.** Then select **Print Area, Set Print Area.**

Press **Print Preview** again. This time the whole worksheet should be shown.

Press **Print.**

Save and close the worksheet.

Additional exercise

See if you can create a worksheet like the one below to show multiplication tables.

You should only need to enter one formula, like the one in cell F3 below. All the rest can be entered by copying and pasting.

You can practise:

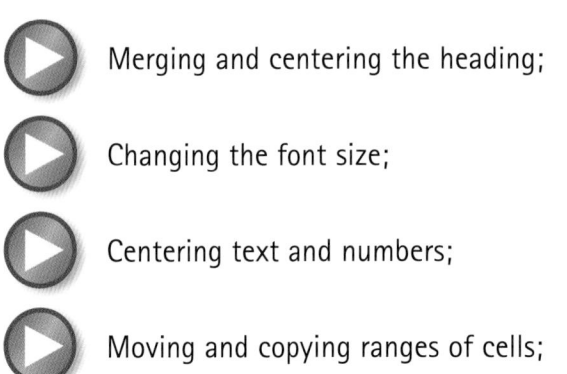 Merging and centering the heading;

Changing the font size;

Centering text and numbers;

Moving and copying ranges of cells;

Adding borders;

 Changing column widths.

You could also try shading cells in different colours if you feel adventurous. Select the cells first and then click the down arrow next to the **Fill Colo**r button and choose a colour.

	A	B	C	D	E	F	G	H	I	J	K	L	M
1							Multiplication Tables						
2													
3		2	x	2	=	4		3	x	2	=	6	
4		2	x	3	=	6		3	x	3	=	9	
5		2	x	4	=	8		3	x	4	=	12	
6		2	x	5	=	10		3	x	5	=	15	
7		2	x	6	=	12		3	x	6	=	18	
8		2	x	7	=	14		3	x	7	=	21	
9		2	x	8	=	16		3	x	8	=	24	
10		2	x	9	=	18		3	x	9	=	27	
11		2	x	10	=	20		3	x	10	=	30	
12		2	x	11	=	22		3	x	11	=	33	
13		2	x	12	=	24		3	x	12	=	36	
14													

Cell F3 = =B3*D3

Figure 8.5

Well done – you have now cracked spreadsheets. Have fun!

Index